# SCIENTISM, MAN, AND RELIGION

# SCIENTISM, MAN, *and* *RELIGION*

## D. R. G. OWEN

*Philadelphia*
THE WESTMINSTER PRESS

PRINTED IN THE UNITED STATES OF AMERICA

*For Two Davids*

# *Preface*

THIS BOOK HAS DEVELOPED OUT
of a course of lectures in Religious Knowledge which has been
given to first year students at Trinity College, Toronto, over the
last five years. Like most teachers, I have found that I have
learned at least as much from my classes as they from me. My
first debt of gratitude is therefore to them. Most of all, they have
taught me the extent of both the interest in and the difficulty of
religious belief in our age. The interest is evidence of the un-
quenchable aspiration of the human spirit. The difficulty, therefore, is due not to anything inherent in human nature, but to
the more or less accidental circumstance of a particular frame
of reference, largely determined by the pre-eminence of science, which has tended to be accepted uncritically in the modern era of Western civilization.

My debt to my own teachers is literally incalculable. What I
have absorbed from them, through their spoken and written
words, has become part of my own thinking, so that I am no
longer able to reckon it up and acknowledge it in detail, but
must in many cases have produced it as though it were my own
original contribution. Others who have a clearer perspective in
relation to this work will recognize the sources of many of its
ideas.

Where I have been conscious of borrowing, I have usually
quoted directly and cited the reference. My thanks are due to
these many authors. I am especially grateful to the following

publishers and authors for permission to quote from their publications as indicated:

Oxford University Press: A. J. Toynbee, *A Study of History.*
Liveright Publishing Corporation: Sigmund Freud, *A General Introduction to Psycho-Analysis.* Copyright, Edward L. Bernays, 1935.
Hogarth Press and Liveright Publishing Corporation: Sigmund Freud, *Beyond the Pleasure Principle* and *The Future of an Illusion.*
Hogarth Press: Sigmund Freud, *The Ego and the Id.*

## Contents

•

# INTRODUCTION

•

# 1

## Science, Scientism, and the " Scientific " Tradition

•

IT HAS BECOME FASHIONABLE IN certain circles to reject the nineteenth century belief in progress as altogether illusory. The course of events in the twentieth century has done much to discredit the assumption that the movement of history is uniformly forward. Nevertheless, there is one kind of progress which, since the seventeenth century, has been real and undeniable. Scientific progress is one of the unquestionable achievements of the modern age.

Modern science began its career as an intellectual expression of that very general demand for freedom which was characteristic of the Renaissance. Science promised to satisfy this demand by adding to man's knowledge and power. In the ensuing centuries this promise has been largely redeemed. Science has enormously increased our knowledge and power, and these are two of the necessary conditions of human freedom. At the same time, it can scarcely be a mere coincidence that the apotheosis of science, which occurred as a result of its benefactions, has been accompanied, in the present century, by the appearance of the mass society in which the vast array of scientific techniques are perversely employed and man's hard-won freedom tends to be eclipsed.

### The Accomplishments of Science

Science itself cannot be blamed for this tragic denouement of the human story in its modern version. Science is actually

13

and, even more, potentially the source of the greatest material blessings that the world has ever known. Wherever it has conducted its researches, it has dissipated the clouds of ignorance and superstition, released men from bondage to unknown and coercive powers, and made it possible for them to become masters in their own world.

The decisively important areas of existence over which the various sciences have helped men to gain control are nature, society, and the psyche. Correspondingly, the sciences are distinguished into the physical sciences, the social sciences, and psychology. As the three areas have come successively under the purview of scientific investigation, the result, in each case, has been more knowledge, more power, and more freedom.

It was the physical universe that first disclosed its secrets to scientific inquiry. Prescientific man remained, for the most part, ignorant of the actual workings of nature. In the beginning he peopled it with spirits and demons to which he was completely and fearfully enslaved. Greek thought, by its attempts at rational explanation, and Christianity, by placing nature in its proper place in the whole scheme of things, to some extent liberated men from this pseudoreligious bondage, and at the same time prepared the way for an objective, scientific study of the physical environment.

The medieval Christian conception of the universe was based on the Aristotelian philosophy of nature and Ptolemaic astronomy. This view, while rational rather than superstitious, was at many points radically mistaken. But since it had been, so to speak, baptized by the Church and incorporated into a Christian philosophy which was thought to be the final and incorrigible truth, no real scientific progress was achieved in the Middle Ages. Consequently, men remained the more or less helpless puppets of natural forces, in no way able to control their physical environment.

The physical sciences, which took their rise in the sixteenth century, radically changed this picture. They discovered certain fundamental laws in accordance with which the universe appears to operate. This knowledge has gone on increasing, and the more man comes to know about nature the more power he has over it. Thus the scientific farmer no longer need submit helplessly to the demands of nature; he has the necessary information and equipment to achieve a considerable degree of dominion over the earth. The scientific doctor is able to exercise a large measure of mastery over nature as it manifests itself in man. Finally, the industrial revolution at the end of the eighteenth century began to put the physical sciences to work on a grand scale in the interests of satisfying the material needs of humanity. Man's power has become steadily greater as more machines and techniques have been introduced. Science has not only freed man from bondage to nature but has now, for the first time in human history, made it technically possible to provide the whole race with much more than a bare material sufficiency.

It is only within certain limits, of course, that science has thus enabled man to manipulate nature for his own purposes. We have not yet discovered all there is to know about nature. And even if our knowledge of natural laws were one day to reach something like completeness, we should still be finite creatures, subject to the limitations of space and time, able to make use of the known laws of the universe but not to claim exemption from their operation.

The social sciences, more recently, have begun to perform the same kind of service in relation to our social environment. To prescientific man his social organization was almost as much of a mystery as the physical world. Primitive peoples tended to deify social powers and slavishly to worship them under symbolic forms such as the totem. Once again Greek and Christian thought, by placing society in its proper perspective, not only began the process of emancipating men from this kind of pseudoreligious bondage but also prepared the way for an objective, scientific study of social forces.

Since this type of scientific inquiry was begun only in the nineteenth century modern man, the lord of nature, tends to remain the creature of the social *status quo*. He is apt to regard it as essentially unchangeable and its norms and standards as absolute. His most cherished beliefs and convictions, as well as his highest ends and values, take shape, not freely and deliberately as the result of conscious choice, but automatically and unconsciously under the great weight of overwhelming social pressures. Man becomes a product of society rather than society a product of man.

In the last hundred years, however, the social sciences have increasingly exposed the nature and operation of these forces. The knowledge that they have accumulated is able by itself to free us; for we have only to become aware of these pressures in order to be liberated from their power. Further, as in the case of the knowledge of nature, the scientific knowledge of sociological laws carries with it the power to direct and control the social structure in accordance with deliberately chosen ends. No longer deriving our values from society as it is, we can entertain a vision of what it might be. Moreover, the various techniques of social engineering enable us to begin the process of transforming the dream into reality.

Again, however, there are limitations that must not be disregarded. The social sciences are far behind the natural sciences in the extent of their knowledge, and no matter how far this knowledge may one day go, it will enable us only to use and not to transcend the laws that it discloses. Moreover, there is a vitally important factor operative in human society and history that must forever remain unknown to science. The scientist, because of the limitations of his method, is incapable of dealing with the human spirit, and therefore can never fully understand the depths and heights of man's social life. Finally, since values and ends belong to the realm of spirit, science itself cannot furnish us with a picture of the best possible society by reference to which its knowledge and power ought always to be utilized.

The third area of existence to which science has most recently extended its investigation is the human soul, or psyche. Prescientific man was ignorant not only of nature and society but also of his own internal psychical organization. Consequently, his character and his whole way of life were apt to be determined for him by a third set of forces which operated within himself but in independence of his conscious control. The modern science of psychology, however, increasingly exposes and describes the unconscious compulsions and coercions that originate from within the psyche. And in this area, even more obviously than in the other two, mere knowledge is by itself able to release us from bondage. Psychoanalysis effects its cures by the simple act of uncovering the source and development of the neuroses. Further, on the level of power, the science of the psyche furnishes a set of techniques, as well as therapeutic practices, that can help us to control the psyche and shape the character in accordance with our ideas of what man ought to be.

The claims that we make here must, once again, be carefully qualified. The first qualification is the same as that which applies to the other sciences: no matter how complete our scientific knowledge may eventually become (and it is still extremely limited in the case of psychology), we shall remain finite creatures, working within and not above the context of the laws that we have discovered. Secondly, it is important to understand that the psyche, which is the object of scientific investigation, is by no means identical with the human spirit.[1] The reaches of the spirit are hidden from scientific investigation, and, therefore, man, in the deepest level of his being, stands beyond not only the control but also the understanding of science in itself. Finally, since science cannot concern itself with values that belong to the level of the spirit, it can tell us nothing of the ideal self which is the real end for which the knowledge and techniques of psychology ought to be employed.

Bearing in mind the limitations that apply to the various sciences, we can readily recognize the impressive and indispensable contributions that they have made to human knowledge, power, and freedom. Scientific knowledge in all its forms emancipates us from servitude to the unknown forces of nature, society, and the psyche. Scientific power enables us, within limits, to utilize the forces of nature, to control the social structure, and to direct the psychical apparatus in accordance with the highest ends and purposes. These achievements are the true glory of a scientific age.

## The Principles of Science

The limitations of science are inherent in its principles and it is the scrupulous adherence to these principles that is responsible for its outstanding successes.

There are four basic principles that serve to define the essence of genuine science. The first is *the empirical principle,* which refers to the method of science. This method of investigation begins with observations and experiments carried out over a long period of time and in carefully controlled situations. The next step is to formulate a hypothesis as the possible explanation of the facts that have been ascertained. The scientist then proceeds to deduce what ought to happen if the hypothesis is true. And finally he returns to observation and experiment in order to discover whether the predicted consequences do in fact occur. The empirical principle of science is a stipulation to the effect that no belief is to be regarded as *scientific* unless it can be tested by this method. This is simply a limiting principle defining the nature of scientific beliefs; nothing whatever is said about the possibility of other methods or the validity of other classes of beliefs.

The second basis of science is *the quantitative principle* which follows necessarily from the first. Since the scientific method begins and ends with observation, science can concern itself only with that kind of reality which is observable; and the kind of reality that can be observed is *physical* reality. Science also aims at mathematical exactitude and therefore restricts its investigations to that kind of reality which is measurable; and the kind of reality that can be measured is *quantitative*. We can measure, for example, the size, but not the beauty, of a picture; we can observe the physiological aspects, but not the goodness, of a human action. The quantitative principle is a limiting principle which states that as long as science is true to its method it must confine its studies to the observable and measurable aspects of reality. Again, nothing whatever is said about the possibility of other aspects of reality which might be known in different ways. The fact that spirit and values are intangible and immeasurable means, not that they are unreal, but that they fall outside the scope of scientific investigation.

The third principle has to do with the goal of every scientific inquiry. We may call it *the mechanical principle*. Science aims at formulating the general laws that govern the behavior of events in its field. But a general law is applicable only to events that happen in regular, repeated, and invariable sequences. We arrive at the law that water boils at 212° Fahrenheit because in our experience the heating of the water to this temperature is always followed by its boiling; the water has no choice in the matter — the same cause is always followed by the same effect. Only those events that happen in this way are amenable to treatment in terms of general laws. The mechanical principle is a limiting principle which recognizes that science, because it is concerned with laws, is restricted to the study of that kind of behavior which consists of natural cause-and-effect series. Once more it should be noted that nothing is said by science about the possibility of another kind of behavior, such as free, unique, unrepeatable acts which, as far as science is concerned, may certainly occur but do not come within the range of scientific explanation.

The scientific method is, as it were, a pair of spectacles, the two lenses of which are the quantitative and mechanical principles. Whoever wears these spectacles will be able to see only what they permit him to see. Thus the scientist must interpret everything which he studies in quantitative and mechanical [2] terms. This means, as the genuine scientist recognizes, not that everything is quantitative and mechanical in nature but rather that his researches are restricted to these aspects of reality. He understands that in so far as reality is more and other than these aspects his theories are abstractions; they deal not with reality as a whole but with certain abstracted features of reality.

The fourth fundamental characteristic of science may be

called *the progressive principle*. The method of science is such that this is one of the few human enterprises that is infinitely self-correcting. No scientific theory is regarded as final. Every hypothesis that science arrives at is liable to constant revision and even rejection in the light of future experience. This means that its theories are constantly being refined and its techniques steadily improved. Moreover, the scientific store of information and skills is not only always expanding but is normally available to all investigators, and every scientist stands on the shoulders of his predecessors. This is what it means to say that science is genuinely and essentially progressive. This progressive principle of science, however, contains no implication about progress on other levels of life; in itself it is no guarantee of *human* progress.

These four principles, the empirical, quantitative, mechanical, and progressive, are not only perfectly valid as the limiting and working principles of science, but they are also responsible for the enormous achievements of science in the modern age.

## The Dogmas of Scientism

The successes of science are due to its careful observance of its limitations. It confines itself to the quantitative and mechanical and does not presume to speak about spirit, values, and freedom; it understands that there may be vast areas of reality that lie beyond its reach. Science, however, because of its accomplishments, has acquired tremendous prestige and has risen in spite of itself to a position of predominant authority in our age. As a result of this exaltation science, in some quarters, has come to be worshiped as omniscient, omnipotent, and the bearer of man's salvation. Such an attitude to science is, of course, entirely unscientific. It must be carefully distinguished from science proper. We may call it scientism or scientolatry. This peculiarly modern form of idolatry refuses to recognize the limitations of science and claims that its working principles can be used as universal principles, in terms of which the *whole* of reality can be explained and controlled. Scientism thus transforms the limiting principles of science into all-embracing dogmas which are regarded as absolute and final truths.

Scientolatry, therefore, claims that it can solve *all* problems " scientifically." Unlike genuine science, it does presume to examine the questions of spirit, values, and freedom; and, in every case, its verdict is negative. The quantitative principle becomes the dogma of materialism or naturalism, which denies the reality of spirit and the objectivity of values. The mechanical principle becomes the dogma of determinism, which denies the reality of freedom. At the same time, the depressing implications of these conclusions are avoided by the transformation of the progressive principle of science into the dogma of utopianism, which supposes that the coming of the ideal society is guaranteed by science and evolution.

The interesting and ominous point is that it is just these dogmas that we discover, in various versions, at the basis of the ideologies of both Communism and Nazism. And we know that the social and political fruit of these ideologies is totalitarianism — the modern slave state. If scientism is what we mean when we describe the modern age as " scientific," then it is true to say that totalitarianism is what a " scientific " age deserves. But we must be careful always to realize that it is scientolatry, and not science, that is the villain of the piece.

Scientism, in several varieties, is a conscious and easily identified philosophy which, since the seventeenth century, has turned up at certain definite times and places. We can expose, isolate, and quarantine the phenomenon. This is the course that we followed recently in relation to Nazism and that we are now pursuing in relation to Communism. But what if we were to discover that we ourselves had all along been infected by the same disease, of which these ideologies were only the most virulent form and the totalitarian society the most obvious symptom?

The fact is that, in addition to science on the one hand and scientolatry on the other, there is a much more intangible, pervasive, and unconscious influence in Western society which stands, so to speak, midway between the two. This is a vague climate of opinion or intellectual atmosphere which, in our age, has also taken shape under the influence of science. Every civilization or period of history has some such over-all frame of reference, which we may call the *tradition* of the age. It consists of certain assumptions, presuppositions, or axioms that are more or less unconsciously *taken for granted*. They form the general context, the validity of which is for the most part unexamined, within which all questions tend to be raised and answered. The assumptions are borrowed, with a greater or lesser degree of distortion, from the basic principles of that element in the culture which has acquired the greatest prestige. The principles in question are distorted into loose generalizations, which then proceed to determine, to a very large extent, the character of all the other elements in the culture. Thus the prevailing tradition, with its general presuppositions, exercises an important influence on the development, not only of the typical philosophy of the era, but also of its political institutions, its economic arrangements, its morals, art, and literature.

The climate of opinion in the Middle Ages consisted of axioms which were derived from the religion of the period. The age might, therefore, be described as the "catholic" age and its tradition as the "catholic" tradition — even though its prevailing assumptions were by no means faithful reflections of actual Catholic doctrine. Similarly, the tradition of the modern age, beginning with the sixteenth century, has borrowed its characteristic presuppositions from the science of the time and consequently might be called the "scientific" tradition — even though its axioms are generalized distortions of the valid principles of true science. This is still another sense in which the modern period of Western civilization is known as the "scientific" age.

The expression "scientific age" has three different referents, each of which is related to, but must be scrupulously distinguished from, the other two: first, there is science itself with its limiting principles; secondly, there is the "scientific" tradition with its general assumptions; and thirdly, there is scientism or scientolatry with its universal dogmas. The fatal passage from the first to the third can be explained only by examining the second of these phenomena.

The connection and difference between the valid principles of science and the illicit generalizations of the "scientific" tradition can be easily indicated. First, the empirical principle, which simply stated that a belief in order to be *scientific* must be testable by the scientific method, becomes in the tradition *the empiricistic axiom,* which is the tendency to assume that a belief in order to be *respectable* must be scientifically verifiable; the limiting character of the principle is forgotten and the scientific method is regarded as the only reliable method of arriving at any kind of truth. Secondly, the quantitative principle of science merely pointed out that science because of its method can deal only with the measurable aspects of reality; the "scientific" tradition transforms this stipulation into *the materialistic axiom,* which is the tendency to assume that, since the scientific method is the only true method of knowledge and is restricted by definition to what can be observed, the physical is the only kind of reality that we can genuinely come to know. In the third place, the mechanical principle, which declared that science because it aims at the formulation of general laws must confine itself to regularly repeated sequences, is changed into *the mechanistic presupposition,* which takes it for granted that real knowledge is restricted to knowledge of mechanical behavior. Finally, the progressive principle of science, which has to do with the constant improvement of scientific theories and techniques, becomes *the optimistic assumption,* which is the tendency to suppose without question that men and all their works are steadily advancing and that in the not too distant future science by itself will bring them to perfection.

These four axioms have become the substance of the intellectual atmosphere of the "scientific" age. They have colored our way of thinking and our whole way of life. This fact accounts for the paradoxical and tragic reversal in which an age that began by crying out for more freedom, and, with a view to satisfying that aspiration, created the great instrument called science, ends by producing the mass society in which scientific knowledge and techniques are prostituted and human freedom compromised. For the assumptions in question only have to be made explicit and taken to their logical conclusion in order to result in a dogmatic scientism of which the Marxist philosophy with its materialistic and deterministic doctrines is the prime example, and the totalitarian state with its dehumanizing and enslaving tendencies the inevitable offspring.[3]

In our society, the presuppositions of the "scientific" tradition have operated for the most part as a half-conscious and unexamined way of looking at things. Where they are rationally elaborated in the West, they take the form of a pragmatic scientism which aims at a totally industrialized, technological, "scientific" society. This is the direction in which we often appear to be moving. If the aim were fully realized, the result would be a Western version of the mass society in which the fate of the individual would be scarcely less hideous than that which has befallen him in the contemporary totalitarian state.

It cannot be too often insisted that it is not science that produces the mass society. On the contrary, by furnishing the necessary material conditions in the shape of knowledge and power science can help to make men free. But when the limits of science are disregarded, when science becomes an absolute authority, when its principles are first converted into the generalized assumptions of a prevailing tradition and then articulated in the all-embracing dogmas of a pseudoscientific metaphysics, then men find themselves, at the end of the scientific age, not free but enslaved in new and more terrible forms of bondage.

PART

I

•

# SCIENTISM, MATERIALISM, and COMMUNISM

# 2

## Materialism and Sociology

•

ONE FORM THAT SCIENTISM
takes is a materialistic metaphysics which, in its modern versions, begins with Hobbes and ends perhaps with Marx. In all
the guises that it assumes in this period, the general assumptions of the "scientific" tradition become forthright and unambiguous dogmas. The most important modification that materialism undergoes in the course of its development between
Hobbes and Marx is that the former is mainly concerned to
construct a theory of reality on the basis of physics, whereas
the latter, while retaining the materialistic foundation, is preoccupied with the science of society. For it is the nineteenth
and twentieth century scientolators who most of all demand
of their god that he save mankind, and it has become clear by
this time that the physical sciences by themselves are incapable of fulfilling this messianic task.

Scientism must, therefore, look elsewhere for its savior,
though not, of course, beyond the bounds of science. It was
Auguste Comte who laid the foundations of a sociology that, as
he hoped, by applying the methods of the physical sciences to
the problems of man, would provide the blueprint for the perfect society on earth. And it is the combination of materialism,
"scientific" sociology, and utopianism that is the essence of
the Marxist creed.

### Hobbes and Materialism

Thomas Hobbes, an English philosopher of the seventeenth
century, was the first scientolator. Scientists like Copernicus,

27

Kepler, and Galileo had revolutionized the concept of nature. Isaac Newton was working out his great scientific theory of the physical universe as entirely explicable in terms of atoms moving in accordance with certain mechanical laws of motion. What Hobbes did, setting the pattern that scientism has followed ever since, was to turn these hypotheses, which applied only to nature, into dogmas which applied to the whole of reality.

Physics is interested only in matter in motion. Hobbes said that reality, including man and all his functions, was matter in motion and nothing more. Seventeenth century science discovered that matter moved in accordance with mechanical law. Hobbes insisted that all activity, including human behavior, could be explained in the same way. Hobbes's basic dogma, then, was that all reality is physical in essence and mechanical in behavior.

The theory is obviously applicable to the material universe. But in applying it to man there are serious difficulties. First of all, the fact of human consciousness does not, at first sight, appear to be explicable in terms of mere matter in motion. Hobbes made a brave attempt to overcome this problem. The mind, he said, is nothing but the brain. Consciousness is made up of sensations and ideas. Sensations are nothing but motions in the physical brain caused by the impact upon it of motions coming from external objects. When these motions continue in the brain, in accordance with the first law of motion, we call them ideas. Thus, consciousness, both as sensation and as idea, is simply matter in motion.[1]

The second problem which confronted Hobbes was connected with human behavior. Can a human act be fully explained in terms of the laws of motion? Hobbes's answer is an ingenious affirmative. The first stimulus to an action occurs when motion coming from an external body impinges on a human body's internal motion which consists of pulse, breathing, and similar involuntary activity. The result is that the internal motion is either facilitated or impeded. When it is facilitated, pleasure ensues, when impeded, pain. Pleasure develops into motion toward the external body and is the beginning of appetite or desire; pain becomes motion " fromward " and is the beginning of aversion or fear. Finally, desire issues in " pursuit " of the object, fear into " avoidance," and an action takes place.[2]

All man's behavior is thus ultimately due to the same laws of motion which govern the universe and which, in the case of man, exercise their power through the feelings of pleasure and pain, desire and fear. The notions of freedom, responsibility, and the will are deliberately excluded, as illusory, in order to subsume human conduct, like human consciousness, under the department of physics. The so-called free and deliberate decision of the will is just " the last appetite or aversion " in " the whole sum of desires, aversions, hopes and fears . . . that we call deliberation."[3]

A third difficulty for Hobbes was the apparent reality of values which do not appear to be reducible in nature to matter in motion. What are the ultimate referents of value terms like " good " and " right "? Hobbes's answer is that good is simply the term which we apply to objects we desire, and the ultimate good, which is power, is what we desire above everything. Human life is chiefly characterized by " a perpetual and restless desire of power after power that ceaseth only in death."[4] As for the ideas of right and wrong, there are no natural moral standards known to man: " the notions of right and wrong, justice and injustice, have there no place."[5] Ethical norms only come into existence with, and are determined by, society; and like society they are artificial and conventional in nature.

The value term " good " is thus reduced by Hobbes to mean " whatever is desired," which in the end is always power; the meaning of the term " right " is decided by society and therefore varies as societies vary.

It is Hobbes's analysis of human nature that leads him to advocate a totalitarian type of society. Since each man desires power for himself, life, in its natural state, is " a war of every man against every man . . . and the life of man, solitary, poor, nasty, brutish, and short."[6] Man, by nature, is a brute, entirely at the mercy of his appetites and dominated by the lust for power. The only way to domesticate him is to establish the absolute state, which is alone strong enough to impose peace and order on this amoral, contentious, and anarchic animal.

According to Hobbes, once it has come about that men, in order to escape from the intolerable conditions of their natural state, have agreed unconditionally to obey a central political authority, that authority, preferably vested in one man, ought to be regarded as absolutely sovereign. It alone determines what is right and wrong and there can therefore be no appeal against it on "moral" grounds. It also decides what beliefs are valid and invalid and is thus the arbiter of what is true and false. In addition, the sovereign power has complete control over the person and property of all citizens and over the activities of all groups within the body politic. It can imprison and punish arbitrarily, can confiscate and distribute whatever and however it wishes, and can declare war and peace as it sees fit. In a word, this is the totalitarian state.[7]

In the doctrines which Hobbes elaborated to explain human consciousness, behavior, and values, we can clearly see the results of attempting to apply the assumptions of the "scientific" tradition to man in universal and dogmatic fashion. His account of consciousness obviously stems from the materialistic presupposition and his deterministic explanation of human action from the mechanistic axiom of the "scientific" climate of opinion. Similarly, his efforts to reduce the meaning of the great value word "good" to a "natural" meaning and to explain ethical standards as entirely relative to society must be understood against the background of his materialistic and deterministic dogmas.

The philosophy of Hobbes is a vivid illustration of the way in which the materialistic denial of the nonmaterial in man, the deterministic denial of human freedom, and the relativistic denial of universal values are all logically implied in scientism. The significant point is that, for Hobbes at any rate, totalitarianism was the natural political corollary of these doctrines.

If man is not by nature a free spirit, not governed by objective, universal standards or oriented toward eternal values, but rather an unruly animal driven by fear and lust, then the absolute state would appear to be both his appropriate political context and also his only hope of an orderly and stable existence. Is there, perhaps, an inherent connection between scientism, on the one hand, with its typical doctrines of man, and totalitarianism, on the other, which simply puts these doctrines into practice?

## Comte and Sociology

The influence of the "scientific" tradition on Comte, a French philosopher of the first half of the nineteenth century, is apparent, to begin with, in the name that he gave to his philosophy. The name "positivism" stands for the empiricistic axiom which assumes that *all* knowledge is derived from phenomena presented to the senses. In Comte this becomes a dogma: "true observation" is "the only possible basis of such knowledge as is really within our reach"; real knowledge is thus limited to what we can observe, that is, to science, but this is "quite sufficient for all our true requirements." [8]

Genuine science recognizes that its knowledge is restricted to theories that can be tested by observation; this is the empirical principle. The empiricistic assumption of the "scientific" frame of reference takes it for granted that this must be the criterion of all beliefs. Scientism, as in Comte, turns this into the dogma that science alone achieves real knowledge. According to Comte, the intellectual history of man can be divided into three stages of development: first, the theological stage, in which everything was explained in terms of supernatural causes; second, the metaphysical stage, in which everything was explained in terms of essences or forms; and third, and last, the positive stage, in which man comes to understand everything in terms of scientific laws. This final stage, represented by the reign of science, means truth and salvation for the human race.

By the time that Comte was writing, science had already

been in the ascendant for a considerable period, and yet there were many problems that appeared to be no nearer to solution. This was due, he said, to the fact that science had still not turned its attention to human society. If science, as well as studying the physical world, were to apply its methods to the political and economic realms, the remaining difficulties would soon be overcome.[9]

Comte himself attempted to construct a scientific sociology on the basis of his analysis of man's intellectual development. Corresponding to the theological stage was a priestly type of society, and to the metaphysical a juristic type. Now, in our time, the scientific or positive stage has produced an industrial society. The problem is to organize this society on scientific lines, so as to produce a new scientific social order. The new scientific society, he said, will be the offspring of the marriage of the "great idea," which of course is positivism, with the "great force," which is the "proletariate." [10]

Comte's great contribution to human thought was his idea of a science of society, or scientific sociology, which, in the hundred years since his death, has added greatly to man's knowledge. But it was a serious misfortune that this idea was introduced by a man who was not a scientist but a scientolator; the social sciences, ever since, have had the greatest difficulty in freeing themselves from the dogmas of scientism.

Sociology, in order to be a science, must operate on the basis of the principles of science; it must restrict itself to those aspects of human society that are quantitative and that can be described in terms of general laws. But Comte and his followers proceeded on the basis of the generalized assumptions of the "scientific" tradition, which they turned into absolute dogmas. Those aspects of society that scientific sociology investigates are the only aspects there are, and therefore human society can be *fully and completely* explained in materialistic and deterministic terms. Comte liked to speak of his new science as "social *physics*," thereby betraying his conviction that a society of men can be studied in exactly the same way as a society of atoms. Just as Hobbes thought that physics could be extended to include man, so Comte hoped that it could be widened to embrace society. Moreover, on the basis of the optimistic presupposition, which is a generalization of the progressive principle of science, he was convinced that the scientific study of society would speedily produce utopia.

There is nothing new in the fact that Comte looked to science for all truth; this is simply the dogmatic version of the empiricistic bias of the prevailing climate of opinion. What was new was his conception of a science of social behavior which would employ the methods of the physical sciences to introduce the perfect social organization. It was in this notion, as well as in the designation of the proletariate as the bearer of supreme political power, that he prepared the way for Marx.

## Hostility to Religion

Another characteristic that is common to all forms of scientism is hostility to the Christian religion. Hobbes refrained from attacking it openly, since in his day the Christian tradition was still powerful enough to discourage aggressive atheism. Hobbes actually gave the Church a place in his State, with the proviso that, like all other institutions in the totalitarian system, its beliefs and practices must be entirely under the control of the absolute sovereign power.[11]

Atheism is nevertheless implied in the metaphysics of Hobbes. The dogma of materialism does not admit of the reality of the spirit. If spirit, he said, is supposed to stand for an "immaterial substance," it stands for nothing at all. Such an expression is a contradiction in terms, like "incorporeal body."[12] He went on to give the familiar account of the origins of religion, which is supposed to establish its fallacious character: primitive man does not understand the real causes of events in nature and therefore ascribes them to invisible powers;[13] the implication is that all religious belief is superstition of this kind and that it will gradually disappear as science discovers the true explanations of natural phenomena.

Comte agreed that religion belongs properly to the earliest

stage of man's intellectual development, and that it will disappear when science provides the solutions of reason for those problems to which religion advances the answers of superstition. Comte gave no explanation of the fact that by the time he was writing the Christian religion had survived three centuries of science. But he found in this fact a further explanation of the continued troubles and turmoils of man in the great positivistic age. In such an age the discredited religious attitude is a dangerous anachronism, for it comes into conflict with the new revelation furnished by science. The only solution is the final abolition of the old religion and the complete triumph of science. Science must replace religion as the dominant influence in human society.[14]

Eventually, however, Comte came to see that science by itself is too cold, technical, and impersonal to satisfy the religious needs of men. If we replace God by the state, as Hobbes in effect suggested, then patriotism perhaps can fill the vacuum. But if we replace God by science, as Comte at first proposed, where can we find an object of *worship?* Comte's answer was "humanity." After all, it was man who, through his science, was now achieving truth and salvation, just as it was God who, in the old religion, was supposed to be the author of revelation and redemption. The traditional ritual, sacred calendar, and all the paraphernalia of religion must simply be revised so as to make humanity the object of their veneration.[15]

The dogma of materialism, which is basic to scientism, entails the rejection of all that is nonphysical, whether it be the human spirit or universal values or God. Scientism is, therefore, faced with the problem of explaining man's age-old belief in their reality. Since the truth of such beliefs would destroy the basis of this philosophy, the only way in which it can satisfactorily explain them is to explain them away. Human consciousness is therefore reduced to matter in motion, human values to power and social convention, and human religion to primitive mistakes and ignorance.

Karl Marx, of course, inherited this hostility to religion that is characteristic of scientism. He took over Hobbes's account of its origin and supposed, with him and with Comte, that this was sufficient to disprove its validity. But he was more interested in discovering and removing the causes of its survival, which Comte had not succeeded in doing. It is interesting to notice, however, that religion continues to exist in the actual Marxist state of today, and that it does so in both of the forms recommended by Hobbes and Comte. In the first place, the Christian Church is allowed to function, but only under the rigid supervision and direction of the State, in exactly the way foreseen by Hobbes. And, secondly, Communism has itself become a kind of humanistic religion, very much after the fashion suggested by Comte.

# 3

## Marxism and the Communist Society

•

THE PHILOSOPHY OF KARL MARX, formulated in the middle of the nineteenth century, is the most systematic exposition of the materialistic type of scientism and the most consistent application of its dogmas to the problems of human society. Marx, however, unlike Comte, was not only a scientolator but also a genuine social scientist. His writings, therefore, are a curious blend of pseudoscientific metaphysics and serious sociological analysis.

Marx's rigorous application of the scientific method to the study of the nature, history, and problems of human society could not but result in increased understanding and control of the social environment. Whatever may be thought of the movement to which Marxism has given rise in the twentieth century, it cannot be denied that the mass of sociological data that Marx collected and the brilliant theories that he elaborated have opened the way to new knowledge and power in the social field and are among the most important achievements of this century.[1]

On the other hand, Marx, as a typical child of the "scientific" age, tended to disregard the limitations inherent in the principles of science and to turn the general assumptions of the "scientific" climate of opinion into universal and final truths.

### Marxism

The first principle of science is the empirical principle. The scientific method begins with observed facts, forms hypotheses on the basis of these facts, and tests the hypotheses by a return

36

to observation. In the "scientific" tradition the principle that all *scientific* theories must be testable in this way becomes the assumption that this is the *only* path to genuine knowledge. This assumption manifests itself again and again in the writings of Marx. He could think of no higher recommendation for his sociological theory than to call it "scientific socialism" and to describe its philosophical basis as "the real, positive science." [2] Similarly, Lenin said that Marxism was "true to all the teachings of natural science" and that "the historic materialism of Marx is one of the greatest achievements of scientific thought." [3]

While Marx thus took over the empiricistic axiom, the fact that he proceeded to transform the remaining presuppositions of the prevailing tradition into explicit dogmas implied the prior abandonment of the genuine empirical principle. Marx himself emphatically denied that in his philosophy there was any departure from this first principle of science. He insisted that he was concerned, not with absolute truth and justice, but only with beliefs that were more true and with a society that would be more just. Nevertheless, the spirit of scientolatry which animated his thinking compelled him to advance his "scientific" materialism and his "scientific" socialism as indubitable certainties. The *Communist Manifesto,* which he wrote in collaboration with Engels, is a model of dogmatic pronouncement; every sentence in it, with the exception of the last, is in the indicative mood and purports to be a statement of unquestionable fact.

Scientism is essentially dogmatic; but it is impossible to be both empirical and dogmatic at the same time, and in the end the method of empirical hypothesis has to be sacrificed. This became quite clear in Lenin, who spoke of Marxism as "all-powerful" and "complete," the "only consistent philosophy" and "the greatest of all instruments of understanding"; he also pointed out, in the same passage, that Marx and Engels "many times explained the profound error of any departure from this foundation." [4]

The empiricistic assumption that science alone gives truth

becomes a dogma to the effect that, in the right hands, it gives absolute and final truths. In Marxism, these truths turn out to be the dogmatic transformation of the remaining axioms of the "scientific" frame of reference. The result is a form of scientism in which the materialistic axiom becomes the doctrine of dialectical materialism, the mechanistic assumption the theory of economic determinism, and the optimistic bias the dogma of the coming classless society.

The second principle of science is the quantitative, which states that the proper field of scientific investigation is the physical realm. In the "scientific" climate of opinion this becomes an assumption that the physical is alone knowable. Two centuries before Marx, Hobbes had developed this into the metaphysical assertion that matter is the only reality. Marx adopted this dogma but developed it in a rather different way. He derived his clue to the interpretation of materialism from another Englishman, this time a contemporary of his own, in the person of Charles Darwin. Marx took over the scientific hypothesis of the evolution of organisms and characteristically applied it to the whole of reality. Matter, or reality, is no longer to be regarded, along the lines of Hobbes, as in motion on analogy with a machine, but rather as developing on analogy with an organism. According to Lenin,[5] matter is "eternally evolving" and this is "evolution in the fullest, deepest, and most universal aspect."

Another influence on Marx's version of materialism was exerted by the Hegelian concept of dialectic. On this view, the process of reality is distinguishable into three stages: first, there is the idea-in-itself (mind); second, the idea-for-itself (nature); and third, the idea-in-and-for-itself (self-consciousness). Within this process as a whole, all secondary developments similarly take place dialectically and invariably pass through the phases of thesis, antithesis, and synthesis. Marx made use of this idea but, as he said, turned it right side up. In the whole evolutionary and dialectical process of reality, nature or matter comes first. Mind or spirit comes second and is merely an evolutionary product and function of matter.

In the three terms, matter (Hobbes), evolution (Darwin), and dialectic (Hegel), we can see both the derivation and the meaning of Marx's dialectical materialism. This materialistic dogma is the basic doctrine of his system. It is a transformation of the materialistic assumption of the prevailing tradition; it clearly denies the primacy and ultimately the efficacy of the spirit both in and over man.

The process of reality, according to Marxism, including the whole history of man, individually, intellectually, and socially, is an evolutionary development and reflection of unconscious matter which proceeds according to known dialectical laws. The main question that concerned Marx had to do with human history, which is the sum total of human thought and behavior. Can man's thought and behavior be explained in exclusively materialistic terms? This is the crucial problem for every form of materialism. Marx's solution was, again, a modification and refinement of Hobbes's theory.

Marxism does not *identify* consciousness with matter in motion, but says that thought is a function or product or reflection of matter: " Man's knowledge reflects a nature existing independently — matter, that is, in a state of development." [6] The development of human thought, down through the ages, reflects the unconscious but dynamic evolution of matter. Therefore, the whole history of man, the social and cultural products of his thinking, is ultimately determined in the same way. Marx himself did try to avoid the dehumanizing implications of too mechanical a determinism. Human history for him was the result of a mutual and reciprocal influence of mind and matter. Material factors determine the general direction of our thinking and the general nature of our ideas; but our ideas again lead us to react to our material conditions so as to change them in certain ways: " Man makes his own history: he does not [however] make it out of conditions chosen by himself, but out of such as he finds close at hand." [7] Men make their own history, but they do so as determined by the existing material conditions. Ultimately, therefore, it is the latter that are the real causes of what men do and think; and the followers of

Marx tend to adopt a more unambiguous determinism which
rejects even the very limited freedom that Marx allowed.

What are the material conditions of life that direct men's
minds and actions? Geographical environment, density of pop-
ulation, and other given natural factors play their part, but the
chief force is the mode of economic production. Marx put it
this way: "What individuals are depends upon the material
conditions of their production. . . . Men are the producers of
their conceptions, ideas, etc. — but this means real, functioning
men, as they are determined by a definite development of their
productive forces." [8] The determinism became more rigid in
Engels: "In every historical epoch the prevailing mode of production . . . form[s] the basis upon which is built up, *and
from which alone can be explained,* the political and intellectual history of that epoch." [9]

This doctrine of economic determinism is the second fundamental dogma of Marxism. Human thought, society, and
culture are the reflections of dialectically evolving matter. Since
these are human works, they are the products of what is material in man. The basic material reality in man is made up of his
material needs and the way in which they are satisfied, and
this latter forms the economic system which accounts for the
whole character of a given period of history.

The same doctrine is employed to explain the transition from
one period to another, and thus to explain the entire course of
human history. Within each period the economic system that
prevails is all-determining. Every economic structure that has
thus far existed satisfies the needs of one class or classes at the
expense of the needs of another class or classes. The latter,
therefore, agitate for, and finally achieve, a change in the economic structure. A change in the economic system gives rise
to a new culture and so to a new historical period. Thus, material needs and their satisfaction not only account for the general
character of an age but also for the way in which the whole of
history proceeds. In the words of Engels:

"The final causes of all social changes and political revolutions are
to be sought, not in men's brains, not in men's better insight into

eternal truth and justice, but in changes in the modes of production and exchange. They are to be sought, not in the philosophy, but in the economics of each political epoch." [10]

Thus the entire course of history is determined and can be explained solely by economic factors, that is to say, material factors in the shape of physical needs and their satisfaction. This is the Marxist dogma of economic determinism applied to history in general and resulting in the economic interpretation of history. The same dogma when applied to the question of values results in the doctrine of ideology, and when applied more particularly to social history, results in the doctrine of class conflict.

Marxism asserts that there is an " ideological taint " in every culture, resulting from its intimate connection with the existing economic system. The culture of a period consists of its political and social institutions, its code of law, its moral standards, aesthetic values, philosophical and religious beliefs. For Marxism, as we have seen, all these are simply reflections of the economic structure. Another way of putting this is to say that all the cultural values of a period are nothing but ideological rationalizations of the existing mode of economic production and exchange. There is no such thing as justice in itself, or goodness, beauty, and truth. What is just and unjust, right and wrong, good and bad, beautiful and ugly, true and false, is really decided, like everything else, by the nature of the economic system. The concepts of justice, goodness, beauty, and truth which prevail in any culture are nothing but standards or conventions shaped and molded by economic considerations. Thus the characteristic values of Greek ethics, politics, art, religion, and philosophy were rationalizations or ideological articulations of the prevailing aristocratic, agricultural, slave economy. Similarly, the values of medieval culture were just " reflections " of the feudal economy of the time, and the typical standards of modern bourgeois culture are nothing but the ideological projections of capitalism.[11] This is the Marxist version of relativism.

The next step in this Marxist doctrine is to point out that one or more classes in a society always benefit to a greater ex-

tent than the others from the existing economic system. Since
these privileged classes have their needs more or less completely satisfied by that economy, they naturally want it to remain as it is forever. They are the champions of the economic
*status quo;* since the existing political, legal, social institutions,
and the ethical, aesthetic, philosophical, and religious values
are the rationalization and ideological justification of the economic structure, they are naturally also the champions and
defenders of the cultural *status quo.* They want it too to remain as it is forever. Precisely because they want the economy
to be regarded as unchangeable, they insist that the relative
and conventional standards of justice, morality, and truth that
happen to prevail in their age are absolute and eternal values;
but in reality the prevailing culture, with its political, ethical,
and intellectual norms, is nothing more than an ideology maintained in the interests of the privileged classes and of the economic *status quo.*

When the principles of economic determinism are applied to
the history of human societies, the result is-the theory of class
conflict. According to Marxism, every economic system, while
it more or less completely satisfies the needs of some classes,
leaves the needs of others relatively unsatisfied. Just as the
privileged classes naturally espouse the *status quo,* the underprivileged or exploited classes inevitably agitate for a change
in the mode of production and exchange. Consequently a struggle between classes ensues, and a dialectical process begins
which is the reflection, on the historical plane, of the universal
dialectical evolution of matter. In this historical dialectic the
thesis is the privileged classes, the antithesis is the exploited
classes, and the synthesis is achieved when one of the latter
revolts and itself assumes a privileged position by introducing
modifications or a complete renovation of the economy. This
change does not, however, eliminate the class conflict, but
simply constitutes a change in the positions of the respective
classes. The new privileged class continues the exploitation of
the other classes, and the synthesis becomes a new thesis, giving rise to an antithesis, and the historical dialectic proceeds.

This is the Marxist account of the evolution of societies, reflecting the dialectical evolution of matter in general. " The whole history of mankind hitherto . . . has been a history of class struggles, contests between exploiting and exploited, ruling and oppressed classes: the history of these class struggles forms a series of evolutions." [12] Thus Darwin's scientific hypothesis of organic evolution is applied as a dogma to the historical process as a whole.

The dogma of economic determinism, with its corollaries in the economic interpretation of history, the ideological explanation of values, and the class-conflict theory of society, is meant to be a full and final account of the whole of human culture and history. This deterministic dogma is, of course, the transformation of the general mechanistic presupposition of the age, which is, in turn, a distortion of the third, or mechanical, principle of genuine science. In the characteristic fashion of scientism, it carries with it a radical depreciation, if not denial, of human freedom and a relativistic reduction of human values. All the great edifices of intellectual, social, and artistic achievement, which we like to ascribe to the genius of the free human spirit in its pursuit of truth, beauty, and goodness, become the more or less automatic reflections of the various modes of economic production.

Another axiom of the " scientific " age, which is a generalization of the fourth, or progressive, principle of science, is the optimistic assumption that progress on every level of life is the law of human history. This idea, which was widely entertained in the nineteenth century, was developed by Marx into the dogma of the coming classless or perfect society.

In the modern capitalistic era, according to Marx, the class conflict is carried on between the capitalist class, which is the privileged, exploiting class, and the proletariate, which is the oppressed and exploited class. Thus the two terms of the dialectical tension in our society are the capitalist class or *bourgeoisie* (thesis) and the working class or proletariate (antithesis). The synthesis will be achieved when the proletariate revolt, oust the *bourgeoisie,* and take over their privileged position.

This revolution, however, will be different from all those that have previously occurred. The triumph of the proletariate will not, as always before, generate a new class conflict, but on the contrary will be the final and permanent synthesis resulting in the final and perfect stage of social evolution. There are two reasons why the proletarian victory cannot lead to renewed class conflict and exploitation but rather brings to an end the dialectical process of history. In the first place, the proletariate is "the immense majority," [13] and its victory will therefore be the victory of mankind. The dialectical tension in society (or class conflict) has never before been so clear-cut. Hitherto there have always been, not just two classes struggling with each other, but a great many classes, one of which was most privileged and another of which eventually revolted, succeeded to the most privileged position, and proceeded to exploit the others. In the modern period, however, society has tended more and more to split up into two classes, one of which becomes increasingly smaller and more powerful and the other of which becomes increasingly larger and more exploited until it constitutes the immense majority. The latter, therefore, cannot revolt and free itself without freeing society as a whole, in which case no section of society will remain to be exploited.

"Today the stage has been reached when the exploited and oppressed class — the proletariate — cannot attain its emancipation from the sway of the exploiting and ruling class — the *bourgeoisie* — without at the same time and once and for all emancipating society at large from all exploitation, oppression, class distinction and class struggles." [14]

The second reason for the claim that this revolution will be the end of all class conflict and exploitation is that "the proletarians have nothing to lose but their chains." [15] The proletariate class, unlike all other revolutionary classes in history, has no special interests, the satisfaction of which would lead, in the new order, to the exploitation of others. Thus, when the working class revolts, seizes the means of production, and establishes the dictatorship of the proletariate, it will be the people as a whole who achieve absolute political and economic power.

The dictatorship of the proletariate is not itself the end but only the first step toward the final goal of social evolution. This goal cannot be achieved, simply and directly, by any change, however radical, in the present economic system. The whole structure of capitalistic society and bourgeois culture must first of all be abolished. To this end the proletariate must be thoroughly organized so that it can revolt successfully and gain absolute control of the means of production and of political institutions. This will be the dictatorship of the proletariate, which will be unavoidably totalitarian in character. " The proletariate will use its political supremacy . . . to centralize all instruments of production in the hands of the state, i.e., of the proletariate organized as the ruling class," and, as this quotation from the *Manifesto* goes on to say, " of course, in the beginning, this cannot be effected except by means of despotic inroads." [16]

The totalitarian dictatorship, however, is only a means to an end. Once this stage has been reached, it will be possible to make direct progress to the goal. " When in the course of development, class distinctions have disappeared, and all production has been concentrated in the hands of a vast association of the whole nation, the public power will lose its political character." [17]

The final goal, which is the establishment of Communism proper, in the first place will be free of all class distinctions and conflict. " In place of the old bourgeois society, with its classes and class antagonisms, we shall have an association in which the free development of each is the condition of the free development of all." [18] In the second place, not only will the totalitarian dictatorship be superseded, but there will be no need whatever for any political power or state machinery at all. " Political power, properly so called, is merely the organized power of one class for oppressing another." [19] Since the Communist society will be classless, the political machinery of the state will not so much be abolished as, in Engel's phrase, just "wither away." [20] In the third place, according to Marx, in the classless, stateless Communist society wealth will be distributed, not in accordance with any base principle of self-interest, but in accordance with the formula "from each according to his abilities, to each according to his need." [21]

To describe this vision of the *summum bonum* as "utopian" is clearly no exaggeration. Marxists themselves repudiate the epithet with indignation; but it is difficult to imagine a sociological theory to which it could be more fittingly applied than one which is so optimistic as to suppose that a revolution on the economic level will alter human nature in such a radical way that all social distinctions, political power, and self-interest will disappear.

The utopian tenor of this phase of Marxist theory is reinforced by the claim that the coming of the classless society is absolutely guaranteed. It is insisted that the class conflict as it exists under capitalism will lead *inevitably* to revolution and to the dictatorship of the proletariate, and that this in turn will lead *inevitably* to the establishment of the perfect classless society of Communism. The process is inexorable because determined by the dialectical laws that govern the whole of reality. Thus it is possible for Engels to say that "with the same certainty with which from a given mathematical proposition a new one is deduced, with that same certainty can we deduce the social revolution." [22] The coming of the revolution, the dictatorship of the proletariate, and eventually the ideal society are as absolutely certain as the conclusion of a mathematical deduction. The idea of inevitable progress toward perfection could scarcely be more strongly expressed.

Marxist or materialistic scientism understands that progress in the physical sciences must be matched by progress in the social sciences before mankind can be saved. And as long as the social sciences remain within the materialistic context, they must be heavily economic in their emphasis. This tendency reaches its culmination in Marxism, which gives an exclusively economic interpretation of the whole of history and envisages the final " scientific " society in terms of a perfect economic system. The problems of the human situation having been radically simplified, the solution is comparatively easy. The naïve optimism which is characteristic of a " scientific " age is here transformed into a dogmatic utopianism.

Materialistic or sociological scientism develops the more or less unconscious and haphazard presuppositions of the general " scientific " climate of opinion into explicit, coherent, and interconnected dogmas. The empiricistic axiom becomes a pseudoscientific dogmatism; the materialistic bias becomes the doctrine of dialectical materialism; the mechanistic assumption becomes the theory of economic determinism and ideological relativism; and the optimistic presupposition becomes the dogma of the coming classless society. Materialism, determinism, relativism, and utopianism, in one form or another, are constant elements in every kind of scientism, including that which is prevalent on this side of the Iron Curtain. Marxism simply makes these notions clear and definite, while Communism puts them into practice.

## Marxist Atheism

Hostility to the Christian religion, as one of the normal features of scientism, was already apparent in Hobbes and Comte. In Marx it developed into an aggressive atheism which insisted that religious belief is not only false in its essence but vicious in its effects. Marx agreed with his predecessors that religion finds not only its origin but its fundamental nature in primitive ignorance and superstition. By the nineteenth century, however, this account had lost some of its force. For if it were true, then the scientific explanation of nature, which was now thoroughgoing, should have entailed the complete disappearance of religion. But, in fact, religious beliefs had survived alongside the natural sciences and were even devoutly entertained by many of the foremost scientists themselves. This curious and paradoxical fact, already noted by Comte as a puzzling contradiction, had to be accounted for, and Marx set himself this task.

Religion, he said, has survived in strength, even after the rise of science, because it serves the purposes of the exploiting class.

Like all other aspects of the established culture, religion is utilized by the ruling class in order to hallow the existing social order, and in order to ease the existing social antagonisms. In its function of hallowing the existing order, religion announces that "the powers that be are ordained of God," and are therefore sacrosanct and inviolable. In its function of easing social antagonisms, it provides the exploited class with compensation for their present distress in the form of "pie in the sky when you die." It keeps the underprivileged in their place by teaching them the virtues of meekness, submission, and contentment with their lot, and it prevents them from facing the real facts of their condition by turning their attention to another world. It is in this sense that religion is "the opium of the people." [23] The Church is thus the lackey of the dominant class and will be abolished along with it at the revolution.

Marx, then, advocated, and predicted as inevitable, the complete abolition of religion in every form. Since, like all other evils of human life, it is kept in being by reason of a faulty economic system, it will be destroyed not so much by exposing the illusory character of its beliefs as by removing the causes that underlie its survival, that is to say, by the transformation of the economic system into the Communist society. Marx agreed with Comte that science must replace religion as the controlling factor in human life, and that the controlling science must be the science of social behavior or sociology. Marxist sociology or "scientific socialism" must be the religion of the new age, providing it with its creed, its standards, and its salvation.

Scientism, because of its materialistic basis, cannot admit the validity of any religious belief that is postulated on the reality of the nonphysical. Such belief, it should be observed, is here ruled out a priori, and not as the result of any impartial examination. If materialism is to be maintained, then the universal belief in the reality of the spirit, both in and over man, must be investigated only in order to be explained away. In the type of scientism that reaches its clearest expression in Marx, the essence of religion is explained as a prescientific superstition and its survival as an ideological device employed by the privileged class to help preserve the *status quo*.

As a matter of fact, there is considerable evidence to support both contentions. But the same evidence can be read just as easily to mean, not that religion survives through either ignorance or self-interest, but rather that it is always likely to fall into superstition or exploitation. Which of these interpretations is given depends on one's presuppositions — in the one case the materialistic axiom, and in the other the assumption of the reality of the nonphysical. As between these assumptions, the former tends to be adopted unconsciously in a " scientific " age, but the latter is confirmed by the fact that even " scientific " man appears to be incapable of living by bread alone.

There seems to be an essential element in human nature that cries out for the kind of satisfaction religion alone can give. Comte, who wanted to replace religion with science, found it necessary to introduce his new humanistic religion. Similarly, Communism, which claims to be completely " scientific," develops in fact into a movement that has all the appearances of a religion. And whatever we may think of the crimes which have been committed in the name of theistic religions, we must all agree that they pale into insignificance in comparison with the enormities of this modern humanistic religion.

## Communism

Marxist scientism is, of course, not only a theory; it has borne actual social and political fruit in the form of the contemporary Communist state and the Communist party throughout the world.

It is this twentieth century Communism that has undoubtedly assumed a religious guise. That this should have happened is not surprising. In both Hobbes and Comte, hostility to the superstitions of the old theistic religion led to the introduction of the superstitions of a new humanistic religion; in the one case, the state was worshiped as a god, and in the other it was humanity that was apotheosized. Wherever scientism abolishes God, it erects some idol in his place.

Twentieth century Communism is a religion in the sense that

it has its sacred scriptures, its dogmatic creed, its hierarchy, its promises for the future, and its way of life. Its sacred scriptures consist chiefly of the writings of Karl Marx, which are regarded as the infallible and final truth. The attitude of Communists to these works is fundamentalist in the extreme. Lenin, who occupied the same place in the early days of Communism as Saint Paul in the apostolic age of Christianity, reminded the faithful that there must be no " departure from this foundation." [24] The gospel according to Saint Marx is the final revelation.

If the writings of Marx constitute the Bible of this religion, the *Communist Manifesto* is its creed, the dogmas of which must be accepted without question by the faithful as the ultimate truth. The articles of the creed are the materialistic explanation of reality, the economic interpretation of history, the ideological taint in cultures, the class conflict, the inevitability of the proletarian revolution on a world-wide scale, the dictatorship of the proletariate, and the coming of the kingdom of heaven in the form of the classless Communist society. It has been suggested that just as the Mohammedan creed is summed up in the slogan, " There is no God but Allah, and Mohammed is his prophet," so the Communist creed might be expressed in the slogan, " There is no God, and Karl Marx is his prophet."

The dogmatic creeds of all the world religions are meant not only to be accepted intellectually but also to issue in a certain way of life. This is most emphatically the case in Marxism. Marx insisted that the great object of his philosophy was not so much to understand the world as to change it, or rather to understand it in order to be able to change it.[25] His philosophy is a philosophy of social action, and the Communist religion is a religion of social action. The Communist way of life is a revolutionary way; it is just this fact that transforms the Communist theory into a dynamic religion and its adherents into fanatically devoted zealots, capable of great heights of heroic activity and self-sacrifice. No amount of philosophical criticism of the metaphysical bases of Marxism should obscure the undeniable fact that the genuine Communists have a burning passion for social justice and reform, a deep concern for the poor and the oppressed, and a high ideal of the brotherhood of all men. This passion and this concern and this ideal are reminiscent of the eighth century prophets and of Jesus Christ himself. Communism has a plan for social revolution which aims at the removal of social injustices and inequalities and at the establishment of real brotherhood on earth. This plan, moreover, it attempts to put into practice. The dream of social justice which is the Communist inspiration was born in the manger of the Christian story; but whereas the Christian Church has been too often supine and impotent in the implementation of the vision, the Communist party, whatever we may think of its methods, is at any rate active and dynamic in the pursuit of the goal.

The final religious aspect of Communism is its hierarchy and its discipline. The authority of this hierarchy is absolute; it interprets the creed infallibly in relation to every situation that arises. It decides the "party line," and demands and receives implicit obedience from all the members. The attitude of the Communist to the orthodox Marxist creed and to the unquestioned authority of the party leaders is precisely that of the Roman Catholic to the dictates of the ecclesiastical hierarchy.

If the emergence of a humanistic religion is normal in scientism, the other, not unrelated, development is the inevitable appearance of a totalitarian political system. This development is certainly inherent in the development of Marxism. In the first place, as a materialistic sociology, it is heavily weighted on the side of economics. The assumption is that if the economic conditions of life are perfected, then, in accordance with the doctrine of economic determinism, everything else will follow suit. This means that the nature of the political structure is unimportant, provided only that it is capable of introducing and maintaining the proposed economic system. If it turns out, as in fact it does, that a totalitarian political system is the only one that can perform this task, then such a structure must be imposed; in the Marxist or any other materialistic theory, there are no other considerations which can be brought to bear on the question.

In the second place, totalitarianism is not only accidental but essential in the Marxist plan. According to the *Communist Manifesto*, the revolution will be followed by " the dictatorship of the proletariate "; this dictatorship will have to be exercised, on behalf of the people, by a few men, who will have to " centralize " everything " in the hands of the state "; and " despotic inroads " will be unavoidable.[26]

It is necessary to remember, however, that in Marxism this political dictatorship is not, as in Hobbes and Nazism, the final goal; it is only a preliminary stage on the way. In the end, not only totalitarian power but every kind of state control will disappear. On the other hand, in the contemporary Communist state the " transition stage " appears to have become permanent and it is clearly characterized by all the worst features of totalitarianism.

In any case, even apart from the explicit theories of Marxism on this point, totalitarianism is the logical political consequence of the dogmas of materialism and determinism in whatever form they may appear. For these dogmas deny the validity of universal human values and the reality and freedom of the human spirit; and this denial leads in only one direction.

If the obligation due to universal moral principles is rejected, the only realistic alternative for the maintenance of law and order is that the state should become the absolute arbiter of what is right and wrong. The state, in turn, in making its decisions, can look only to the achievement of its own purposes, the pursuit of which justifies the use of any means whatever. Lies, treachery, ruthlessness, and wholesale murder become entirely respectable provided they serve the ends of the powers that be. This is totalitarian " morality," which simply puts into effect the implications of ethical relativism. Further, if the idea of universal objective truth is abandoned, while it is realized that common beliefs are the only real cement of a society, it follows that the state must also determine what is true and false. Beliefs will be imposed by all the techniques of scientific conditioning and enforced by the ubiquitous activity of the " thought police."

In totalitarianism the state becomes omnipotent, omniscient, the source of all law and of all truth. In other words, the state replaces God. The abolition of God leads to the deification of the state; and the deification of the state results in the abolition of man. For the dogmas of materialism and determinism entail not only atheism but also antihumanism. To deny the primacy of the spirit and the reality of freedom in man is to strip him of his specifically human attributes, to deprive him of his rights, his dignity, his value, and his status as a human person. It becomes quite fitting, then, that the individual should be reduced, as he is in the Communist state, to a soulless cog in a soulless economic machine.

It is scientism that has brought man to this end. It begins by disregarding God and the realm of the spirit; it concentrates attention on the physical world; it interprets man in the materialistic and mechanistic categories that are appropriate to nature; it advocates a " scientific " society in which there is no room for human beings. Moreover, this whole way of thinking, which is simply taken to its logical conclusion in Marxism and put into practice in totalitarian Communism, is also present in the Western world where scientism, in a somewhat more embryonic form, is widely espoused.

# 4

## Sociological Scientism

•

IN ORDER TO DISPROVE THE DOC-
trines of materialistic or sociological scientism it is not enough
to point to the fact that its denial of the spirit, freedom, and
values of man leads logically to totalitarianism. We may heart-
ily dislike the practical conclusions that follow from the theoretical premises, but mere antipathy is no substitute for argument.

In attempting to refute the theories of scientism we can do
two things: First, we can show that its doctrines are not, as
they purport to be, the results of genuine scientific investigation, but rather the inevitable consequences of unproved presuppositions; and, secondly, we can try to prove that the presuppositions, at any rate as applied to human society, are false
to the facts. The first of these points has already been suggested
at one or two places in the previous chapter. It will be further
developed here, along with the second line of argument.

### Criticism of Its Doctrines

The passage from authentic science, with its limiting principles, to a pseudoscientific metaphysics, with its all-embracing
dogmas, can be explained only in terms of the assumptions of
a " scientific " age. It is impossible to understand how the valid
principles of genuine science could have become the false metaphysical doctrines of scientism, unless we realize that the true
scientific spirit has first of all been changed into a general cli-

54

mate of opinion or tradition of life. Modern man, because he owes so much to science, has paid his benefactor the doubtful compliment of transforming its working principles into universal assumptions. Science defines the beliefs that are proper to it in terms of a certain method of investigation; we tend to take it for granted that this empirical method is the only way of discovering truth. Science limits itself to the study of certain aspects of reality; we are apt to assume that these physical and empirical aspects are the only ones that we can really know. Science, so defined and delimited, is essentially progressive; we imagine that progress on every level of life is inevitable.

It is these general assumptions, which constitute the modern pseudoscientific atmosphere of the age, that scientism turns into explicit and all-embracing dogmas: Science alone gives truth and this truth is absolute (the defining dogma of scientism); matter is the primary reality (the dogma of materialism); all behavior, including that of human society, is determined by impersonal forces (the dogma of determinism); all values are simply social conventions (the dogma of relativism); the coming of the ideal society is guaranteed (the dogma of utopianism).

None of these dogmas can be scientifically proved. They can be explained only in terms of the unproved and unprovable assumptions that they articulate. First of all, the assertion that science alone gives truth and gives final truth is obviously not amenable to any possible scientific test, and the latter part of the declaration is a contradiction of the scientific principle which stipulates that all scientific beliefs are merely hypotheses. It is not science but pseudo science that makes claims of this kind on behalf of science. The genuine scientist understands that science neither yields final truth nor provides the only avenue to knowledge. The truths of the poet, the dramatist, the artist, and the lover are arrived at along different lines, but they cannot be dismissed as nothing but illusion.

Secondly, the insistence that matter is the ultimate reality is likewise not the kind of proposition that science is capable of examining, for there is no conceivable scientific method of verification that would be relevant to its truth or falsity. It is, therefore, a pseudoscientific or, at any rate, an unscientific assertion. To anyone who is not committed to the first dogma of scientism, it does not, of course, follow that materialism is false. There are, however, other grounds for refusing to accept this doctrine.

The main difficulty for materialism is that of accounting for the fact of human consciousness in terms of matter in motion and nothing more. Hobbes attempted to identify the mind with the physical brain, and sensation and thought with motion in the brain. This unambiguous identification is impossible for one simple reason: If my sensation of redness were the same thing as the motion in my brain, which undoubtedly accompanies it, then it ought to be possible for a surgeon to open my skull at the moment of sensation and observe it; what he would observe, however, is not my sensation of redness but simply the motion in my brain. This is even more obvious if instead of the sensation of redness I happened to be entertaining the thought that two and two equals four. The fact is that sensation and thought are not the same thing as, though they may never occur apart from, some motion in the brain.

Marx, therefore, avoided the simple identification of mind and matter. Sensation and thought, he said, are "reflections" of matter. Engels pointed out that "mind itself is merely the highest product of matter." [1] There could be no quarrel with these statements if they were simply intended to mean, first, that, as far as we know, thinking is impossible apart from a physical brain, and, secondly, that the human mind has evolved out of unconscious matter. But Marxists clearly think that they are saying more than this; or, rather, they suppose that the declaration of these facts amounts to a proof of the materialistic nature of consciousness. Thus Engels, immediately after the sentence quoted, goes on to say, "This is, of course, pure materialism." The fact, however, that human thinking requires the presence of a physical brain does not mean, as we have seen, that thinking is itself a physical process. And the fact that consciousness has evolved out of what is unconscious no more allows us to define the former in terms of the latter than the fact that modern medicine has developed out of the practices of primitive medicine men permits us to define medicine in terms of witchcraft.

Marxism imagines that it has given a materialistic explanation of thought by calling it nothing but a reflection of matter. But to give a name to X is by no means to explain X. To overlook this obvious fact is to be guilty of an error, characteristic of scientism, that might be called the nominalistic fallacy. We must demand an explanation of the name. We must ask: "What is the nature of this 'reflection'; if it is identical with that which it reflects, why is it necessary to say that it is a reflection *of* matter; and if it is not identical, in what sense is this a materialistic explanation?" Marxism does not answer these questions; because of the materialistic assumption of its "scientific" frame of reference, it takes it for granted that the nature of consciousness must be physical and goes on to the social and cultural questions in which it is more interested.

The idea, never really widespread until the modern period, that the activities of the human mind can be exhaustively described in materialistic categories arises in the following way. Scientists study the physical world by means of their consciousness; it is just because they are conscious beings that they are able to observe external nature. They do not, of course, observe consciousness in the field which they are studying, any more than the absent-minded professor finds the spectacles for which he is searching — because he is wearing them all the time. The scientists, therefore, report, quite properly, that what they observe in their investigations is matter in motion and nothing more. Then a proponent of scientism arrives on the scene and turns this scientific report into a metaphysical dogma covering the whole of reality. He even applies the report, which has to do with what is observed, to the faculty that does the observing, and concludes (though this, of course, was actually his presupposition) that man in no way differs from the rest of nature.

Man, however, does differ from the rest of nature in at least this one respect, that he alone is able to observe, study, and reflect on nature. In order to do this, he must, to some extent, stand outside the physical world, and the faculty by means of which he thus transcends nature cannot be identifiable with nature. Everything that can be observed is, perhaps, explicable in terms of matter in motion, but that which does the observing, and is never itself observable, cannot be explained in this way. To put it differently, man, by virtue of his consciousness, is a subject as well as an object, and as a subject he belongs to a level of reality which is more and other than the realm of natural objects.[2] In short, in human consciousness we come upon a kind of reality that materialism cannot explain.

The third dogma of scientism, which is the theory that all behavior is determined by forces beyond the control of the individual, also cannot be scientifically tested. Science, by reason of its mechanical principle, is restricted to the study of this kind of behavior and hence, in regard to the doctrine of determinism, the possibility of negative instances, which is an essential requirement of a genuine scientific hypothesis, is ruled out a priori. Determinism, as a universal truth, is, therefore, pseudoscientific; it belongs to the area, not of scientific discoveries, but of unprovable presuppositions.

Determinism teaches that the behavior of man is governed in the same way as the rest of nature. It makes no difference whether the processes of nature are pictured on the model of a machine as in Hobbes, or on the model of an evolving organism as in Marx, or whether the ultimate determining factor is thought of as Hobbes's lust for power or as Marx's economic forces; the main point is the same — man is entirely determined by forces beyond his control and human freedom is an illusion.

The main criticism of absolute determinism is quite simple. If man's behavior were entirely determined, then he would never know it; he would be entirely implicated in the net of natural cause and effect and would be unable to rise above it and pass judgment on it. The very fact that a man can insist that all behavior is determined is evidence that he transcends

the whole objective realm, and, to this extent, is free. Only beings who have some freedom are in a position to deny it; animals do not discuss the question.

It is, of course, only absolute determinism that is thus self-
refuting. In regard to a very large area of human behavior, determinism is true. This follows from the degree of truth that is
contained in materialism; whatever else he may be, man is certainly a physical animal, and, to this extent, what he does and
thinks is largely governed by his physical needs and their satisfaction. One of man's natural instincts is the lust for power, and
where this alone is operative, Hobbes's account of human behavior is correct. Another important group of human needs is
the economic, and, therefore, as Marx argued so forcefully, economic factors play a fundamental role in shaping the course of
cultural and social history.

The idea that human life can be *completely* explained in deterministic fashion did not, however, arise from the observation of these facts; it has a less respectable origin. Scientists aim
at the formulation of general laws; they, therefore, confine
themselves to the study of the regular cause-and-effect behavior which can be dealt with in this way. They inevitably
report, then, that what they discover are fixed patterns of
events governed by laws. A philosopher of scientism now appears who takes over this scientific report and applies it universally. When he studies man in terms of this dogma, he concludes, of course (though this was really his presupposition),
that man in no way differs from the rest of nature. But we
know that man does differ from the rest of nature in so far as
he is a self-conscious subject; he is not, therefore, necessarily
governed altogether in the same way as nature; freedom is a
possibility. Further, this freedom is actualized at one point at
least, namely, in the discussion of freedom and determinism,
from which beings who are entirely determined would obviously be excluded.

The dogmas of materialism and determinism are invariably
accompanied by the theory of relativism. For if everything is
matter in motion and if all activity is governed by natural

forces, then it cannot be the case, as men have always thought, that human action ought to be guided by the eternal standards of justice, truth, and goodness or that these values have any objective reality. These ideals have either to be reduced to natural forces such as power, as in Hobbes, or else to be explained as mere social conventions imposed for ulterior purposes, as in Marx. It is obvious, again, that this conclusion follows from previously adopted assumptions and is not the result of impartial investigation. Apart from this fact, relativism in regard to values can be shown to be false in so far as it purports to be exhaustive.

In the first place, the reduction of the term " good " to mean the same as the term " power " (or any other natural phenomenon) runs into insurmountable difficulties. If " good " always means " power," then we ought to be able to substitute the one for the other in every case. But it would be difficult, for example, to see how the voluntary sacrifice of a man's life for the sake of others, which most of us would call good, contributes, in any sense, to the power of the self-sacrificing agent. Further, if " good " always means " power," then the assertion that any kind of power was bad would be a contradiction in terms; but it is certainly at least meaningful to say that the kind of power that the Nazis sought and exercised was bad, and not only for others but also for themselves.

It might be possible to answer this argument by claiming that our idea of what is good and bad is " unnatural," in the sense that it has been foisted upon us by society for purposes of its own. This brings us to the Marxist and more common sociological form of relativism. All values are nothing but social conventions, or, as Marx put it, the ideological rationalization of the *status quo*. On this view, the word " right " in the moral sense means " conforming to the conventions of society." The social sciences have collected an impressive array of evidence to prove that the particular kinds of action that men designate as " right " and " wrong " evince a wide variety from age to age and from society to society. No one denies that this is so, although the extent of the variation is often exaggerated.

What is disputed, however, is the blithe assumption on the part of many social scientists that this evidence is conclusive proof of the relativity of all norms and standards. They overlook the one point that is really significant for a theory of values, and that is the fact, which the same evidence confirms, that all men at all times and in all places have made the distinction between right and wrong and have also been convinced that they *ought to do what is right*. The moral sense itself is an invariable ingredient in human nature and it is one more feature of man that differentiates him from the rest of nature.

In any case, the phrase "morally right" can scarcely be equivalent to "conforming to social conventions," since what is thought to be right by the most morally sensitive people is often precisely the refusal to accept the standards of the time. As a matter of fact, the relativist himself thinks it is right for him to teach relativism, in spite of the fact that to do so is to go against the age-old convention of Western society which holds that there is an objective standard of right and wrong. Actually, the relativist thinks it is right to teach this theory because the theory is true and because it is right to tell the truth. But telling the truth is by no means always the same as conforming to social custom.

A final difficulty for relativism is that truth itself, as a value, must itself be relative. If this were the case, then the theory of relativism could claim to be only relatively and not altogether true. The suggestion, which is often implicitly made, that relativism is absolutely true is, of course, a contradiction in terms. If one wishes to have one's theories regarded as true, one must accept at least one value as real, namely, truth. In this sense, absolute relativism, like absolute determinism, is self-refuting.

This refutation of absolute relativism should not, however, blind us to the valid insights of the Marxist doctrine of ideology. It is probably true that the actual content and meaning of terms like justice, freedom, goodness, beauty, and truth are to some extent determined by the nature of the economic system, and that these values, so understood, are championed by the privileged class, unconsciously, in the interests of maintaining the *status quo.* In every age, there is a tendency to claim absolute and final validity for what are, in fact, only partial and relative comprehensions of true values; and one of the underlying motives is certainly the not always conscious desire to maintain the existing social and economic structure.

One of the weaknesses of the Marxist position is its exclusive emphasis on *economic* self-interest. In fact, of course, there are other forms of self-interest that play their part in tempting man to exalt his relative standards into absolute values. There is, for instance, the lust for power, which Hobbes stressed, and the sexual factor, which Freud singled out; [3] either of these types of self-interest, as well as the economic variety, may be taken as basic, and the choice of any one of them appears to be arbitrary. It is more reasonable to conclude that it is self-interest as such, underlying all these manifestations, that is the real culprit.[4]

Marxism, in its doctrine of ideology, also contains a glaring inconsistency, to which, as it has already been pointed out, relativism is peculiarly prone. If *all* ideas of truth and justice are *entirely* determined by economic factors, then no philosophy can claim to be objectively true and no society objectively just. But Marx explicitly stated that he was seeking ideas that would be " more true " and a society that would be " more just." He must have been assuming here that *his* ideas of truth and justice had genuine validity. The curious fact is that Marx, having rightly criticized all other philosophies and societies for their pretensions to absolute truth and justice, went on to advance precisely the same claims for the Marxist philosophy and the Communist society.

It is only on the basis of materialism and determinism that one is driven into the inconsistencies of absolute relativism. If, on the other hand, we understand that man, because of his consciousness or subjectivity or spirit, transcends nature and has access to another kind of being, it follows that his ideas of truth, beauty, and goodness need not be simply rationalizations entirely determined by material factors and lacking in all validity. These ideas, though always relative and influenced as to their particular content by extraneous circumstances, may be genuine, if distorted, comprehensions of real, objective values that belong to the realm that spirit knows.

A final dogma that turns up in most forms of scientism is the utopian doctrine, which stems from the prevailing nineteenth century assumption of the inevitability of progress. This latter belief, in turn, is an illicit generalization of the progressive principle of science. In Marxism this dogma is expressed in the confident prediction of the coming perfect classless society.

The utopian aspect of the Marxist theory is evident not so much in the nature of the Communist society which man is expected to establish upon the earth as in the means by which it is to be realized. The picture of a society in which there will be no class antagonisms, no state power, and no self-interest, and in which perfect justice and amity will be achieved, is simply the vision of human fulfillment for which men in every age have yearned. The real question has to do with the methods by which mankind is to be redeemed and this *summum bonum* actualized. Marxism finds that the obstacle that stands in man's way is economic in nature. The solution, therefore, is comparatively simple. It is only necessary to abolish economic injustice and introduce the perfect economic system and, *ipso facto*, man himself will become perfectly good; mankind will be regenerated and the kingdom of heaven will be at hand.

The utopian illusion of Marxism is due to the fact that its conception of the ideological taint in human culture does not penetrate to a sufficient depth. It is true that bad economic systems make bad men, but it is also true that, first of all, it is bad men who make bad systems. If self-interest, as such, underlies economic injustice (as well as all other forms of man-made evils), then no economic revolution by itself will overcome and eradicate this fundamental flaw in human nature. Rather, this perversion will remain and will pervert the theoretically most perfect economic schemes. Indeed, if, as Marxism asserts, the regeneration of mankind must wait upon the introduction of the perfect economy, where shall we find the perfect men to establish this system?

Communist theory is also too optimistic when it supposes that the totalitarian political system, which it sees to be necessary in the transition stage, can be superseded in the natural course of development. It is a naïve and superficial view of human nature that does not understand how, in Lord Acton's familiar words, " all power corrupts and absolute power corrupts absolutely." Once a group of men have been vested with such power, it will be difficult, and probably impossible, to persuade them to relinquish it.

Finally, the Marxist failure to apply the doctrine of ideology to the Marxist philosophy is paralleled by a failure to apply the doctrine of dialectical evolution to the Communist society. The dialectical process, when it is being examined for its own sake, is thought of as universal and eternal; its social reflection is the historical development of society, which ought similarly to be unending. Nevertheless, it apparently comes to a full stop with the Communist society. But this is theoretically impossible on Marxist principles. For the final product of social evolution could be only a reflection of the final stage of the whole dialectical process of reality. In other words, it would be the end of the world, which would be a rather startling refutation of the basis of dialectical materialism.

This criticism should not be taken as a derogation of the social ideals enunciated by Communism. It is simply a denial of the utopian expectation that such lofty aspirations can be realized by a humanly contrived redemption of mankind based on a " science " of society that operates entirely within a materialistic and deterministic framework.

### Criticism of Its Atheism

The fixed ideas and prejudices of the prevailing climate of opinion have antireligious implications. If science can give us all truth and power, if matter moving in accordance with general laws is the only kind of reality we can come to know, and if human progress, under science, is guaranteed, then there is already no room for any kind of theistic religion and no need to look for salvation beyond the human level. These implications

are carried to their logical conclusion in the forthright and unambiguous atheism of materialistic scientism.

This atheism is, again, in the first place, not a conclusion arrived at by a careful study of the evidence and the historical
arguments of theology. It is simply the result of the presuppositions of the " scientific " tradition. If reality is investigated
by looking through the lenses of the materialistic and mechanistic spectacles, then, even if there were such realities as God
and the spirit, they could not be discovered by this method of
approach. The investigator will see in his field only those aspects with which his method is capable of dealing. Agnosticism
and atheism are not, as they often claim to be, the necessary
intellectual positions of the scientific mind. They are verdicts
which are determined a priori by the dogmas of scientism.

If we are aware, in advance, of the inadequacy of the presuppositions which lie behind the atheistic position, we can
easily see that the arguments advanced against religious belief
are, in every case, fallacious. First of all, there is the familiar
anthropological account of .the origins of religion which
Hobbes, Comte, and Marx all imagined was tantamount to a
refutation of religious belief. Religion, it is said, arose as a
result of primitive ignorance which led men to ascribe the occurrence of natural events to the activity of spirits. The assumption is that religious belief is essentially this kind of superstitious mistake. In answering this argument, we must point
out, first, that the truth of this description of primitive religion
is itself in question. It has been argued, for instance, that the
earliest religion of man was not " thought out " but " danced
out "; that it was not a quasi-philosophical attempt to *explain*
nature but rather an attempt, by means of mythological stories
and ritual acts, to *express* the reaction of man to the mysterious
elements in his surroundings.[5] It is certainly the case that in the
face of mystery man is ignorant and that *this kind* of ignorance
has its place in the religious response to reality. But it is only
on the basis of the pretentious assumption, not shared by genuine scientists, that there are no essential mysteries but only
problems that we can go on to predict the total substitution of

assured scientific knowledge for all religious faith.

In the second place, even if it were true that religion originated in mistaken theories about nature, it would still not follow that religion, as such, is nothing but this old and outworn superstition. The fact (if such it be) that religion has developed out of superstition by no means proves that it *is* superstition. The fact (if it is a fact) that modern science has developed out of primitive magic does not mean (though we may sometimes be strongly tempted to conclude) that science is nothing more than the old black magic with a new mumbo jumbo. The mistake of supposing that once we have discovered the *origin* of a belief or practice we have destroyed its claims to validity is one of the most common errors of all forms of scientism. We can call it the genetic or "nothing but" fallacy: The final result of a process of development is reduced to its earliest manifestations; the end product is really nothing but the original beginning. Such reasoning has only to be described in order to be dismissed. The fact is, of course, that the way in which a belief or practice arises has nothing to do with the question of its validity. The aboriginal may believe in God because otherwise he cannot account for the lightning; this may be very poor reasoning, but we cannot conclude that *therefore* God does not exist. Yet this is precisely the kind of argument which atheism frequently presents for serious consideration.

The same point can be made against Marx's explanation of the survival of religion in a scientific age. Science has not replaced religion, as we might have expected, because the latter serves the purposes of the exploiting class; it helps to maintain the *status quo* and is therefore simply one aspect of the ideological rationalization of the existing system. Marx assumes that this is further proof of the falsity of religious belief. It is true, of course, that religion is often defended for unsavory reasons. And it cannot be denied that medieval Catholicism often looked like the religious expression of feudalism and that Protestantism frequently appears to play the same role in relation to capitalism. But, again, to suppose that in each case the one is *nothing but* the other is to commit the same kind of fallacy. To suppose that once you have exposed the ulterior purposes for which religion is often propagated you have refuted its claim to truth is to confuse the *causes* or motives of religious teaching with the *reasons* for its truth or falsity. It is clearly a logical fallacy to argue from the nature of the motive behind a belief to some conclusion about its validity. It may be true that primitive man believed in gods *because* of his ignorance of nature and that certain people advocate religion *because* it serves their selfish interests; but neither of these considerations has the slightest bearing on the *reasons* for believing that God either does or does not exist. I may believe that you are a rascal simply because you make more money than I do; but the fact that this is the real cause of my belief is not enough by itself to prove that you are *not* a rascal.

## Sociology as the Key of Knowledge

The type of scientism that can end in Communist totalitarianism is differentiated from other varieties by its prior interest in the " scientific " control of society and by its expectation that utopia will be established in this way.

One of the characteristics of the " scientific " frame of reference or tradition of thought that has been dominant in the modern period is the assumption that the scientific method and the knowledge which it amasses can by themselves bring man to salvation. At one time it was hoped that the physical sciences would be capable of this achievement. Eventually, however, it came to be understood that the knowledge and power that these sciences furnish are just as likely, if uncontrolled, to lead to universal destruction. The question then became: What is there that is capable of exercising the required control? And the answer of materialistic scientism is: *Social* science. The scientific study of social behavior and organization will lead to the building of the perfect society in which all of man's age-old dreams will be fulfilled. Sociology provides the key of knowledge which opens the door to human salvation.

The inadequacy of scientific sociology for the assigned task lies in the implications inherent in its claim to be a science. The term " scientific " means operating on the basis of the scientific method and in allegiance to the fundamental principles of science. These principles are limiting in nature and restrict the scientist to the study of those aspects of his field that are physical and mechanical. When sociology claims to be a science, it is restricting itself in this way. These restrictions obviously have more serious consequences for sociology, which studies the *human* situation, than for the physical sciences, which study the physical world.

The application of the scientific method and its principles to human society is not in question. The social sciences, proceeding in this way, have already achieved great results and will undoubtedly continue to make an ever-increasing contribution to human welfare. The real question is whether this kind of investigation is capable of solving all human problems in the social field and of furnishing the blueprint of the ideal society. This is the claim that is made, not by genuine social science, but by pseudoscientific sociology or sociological scientism.

To suppose that the scientific method can solve *all* social problems is to assume that science can *completely* understand and explain the human situation. This claim could be made only if the limiting principles of science had already been turned into all-embracing truths or, in other words, if science had degenerated into scientism. Science understands that its method restricts it to the study of those aspects of reality that are physical in nature and mechanical in behavior; pseudo science or scientism supposes that the *whole* of reality is of this kind. Similarly, pseudoscientific sociology, instead of recognizing that as long as it is strictly scientific it is limited in its investigations to material factors and to that area of social behavior which can be brought under general laws, insists that the *whole* of human society can be analyzed and controlled under these categories.

Sociological scientism, therefore, does not content itself with acknowledging that the realm of spirit, freedom, and values lies outside its scope, but goes on to deny the reality of all three and to explain them away by various fallacious arguments. Moreover, it claims that its position in regard to these questions is " scientific " and can be " scientifically " proved, whereas in fact it simply follows necessarily from the uncritically accepted presuppositions of the " scientific " age.

Marxist sociology is elaborated consciously within the context of a materialistic metaphysics in which the assumptions of the age become explicit dogmas. It is in Marxism and its fruits, therefore, that we can see most clearly the direction in which sociological scientism leads. This should be a warning against that part of Western social science which tends to slip over, at various points, into scientism of the same general kind. Marxism is entirely true to the materialistic and mechanistic biases when it reduces the individual to an economic unit and finds his appropriate social environment in totalitarian collectivism. If man is nothing but a physical mechanism, entirely determined by his physical needs and the way in which they are satisfied, then it is fitting that he should be treated as an economic cog in an economic machine and that the whole quest for the highest human well-being should become a mere matter of instituting the perfect scientific economic apparatus.

Behind the materialistic and deterministic axioms of scientism in general, and underlying the attempt of sociological scientism to explain the human situation exhaustively in these terms, there lies the assumption that man in no way differs from the rest of nature, as nature is understood by the physical sciences. Professor Toynbee has labeled this notion the " apathetic fallacy ":

" Under the insidious influence of the spirit of an outgoing age we have fallen victim to what we will call the ' apathetic fallacy.' Ruskin warned his readers against the ' pathetic fallacy ' of imaginatively endowing inanimate objects with life; but it is equally necessary for us to be on our guard against the converse error of applying to historical thought, which is a study of living creatures, a scientific method devised for the study of inanimate nature." [6]

It is not only the modern study of history but much of modern sociology that is guilty of this fallacy. And the fallacy, in thi case, is not so much that of applying to human society a method appropriate to nonhuman nature (for such application is proper and often highly enlightening) as that of relying *exclusively* on this method to yield the *whole* truth about man's social life.

When this is done, the inevitable result is that man is regarded as nothing but a physical mechanism. This is not a " scientific " conclusion, as is usually claimed, but is rather the only picture of man that one *can* obtain if one looks at him solely through the spectacles of the scientific method. To imagine that this is the picture of the whole man is to commit the apathetic fallacy. It is to strip man, in advance, of all his specifically *human* attributes and so to prepare the way for his totalitarian fate.

The scientific picture of man is, of course, true as far as it goes. Man *is* an animal, a part of nature, and therefore both he himself and his society are governed by general laws in the same way as the rest of nature. For this reason, the scientific method and its principles can be applied fruitfully to human society. It would be false and foolish to deny the indispensable accretions to human understanding that the social sciences have provided. But when it is supposed that the scientific method is our only source of information about man and his society, then we are on our way to the substitution of an automaton for the human person and of the " scientific " collective for the human community.

If the apathetic fallacy is avoided, then there is no reason to deny, and in fact every reason to affirm, the reality in human life of something we can only describe as spirit. And if the human spirit is real, then there is the possibility of genuine freedom, however limited, and of real values, however dimly comprehended. Finally, if spirit, freedom, and values are authentic and efficacious factors in the human situation, then a sociology that depends *entirely* on the scientific method and mistakes its limiting principles for universal truths will arrive at conclusions that are positively false to the true nature of man's society. Such a sociological scientism, whether of the Marxist or other varieties, will turn out to be not only misleading in theory but disastrous in practice. It can never provide the key of knowledge that will open the door to human salvation. It is much more likely, by depersonalizing man and by collectivizing his society, to lead to perdition.

# SCIENTISM, NATURALISM, and NAZISM

# 5

## Naturalism and Psychology

•

THE SECOND MAIN FORM THAT
scientism assumes differs from the first only in its central preoccupation. It takes for granted in the background both the
axioms of the " scientific " tradition of thought and also the dogmas of a materialistic metaphysics; but it is chiefly concerned
with the implications for *human nature*. It also has something
to say about the ideal society, but its social teaching is, for the
most part, simply a corollary of its doctrine of *man*. In short,
just as human society was the primary interest of materialistic
or sociological scientism, so human nature is the focal point of
naturalistic or psychological scientism.

" Naturalism " is a convenient label to apply to the doctrine
of man that is based on materialistic and deterministic presuppositions. Since Hobbes was one of the first, in the modern period, to employ the dogmas of scientism in general in the analysis of human nature in particular, he re-enters the picture here
as the originator of subsequent naturalistic developments.
Modern naturalism, however, has tended to divide into two
types: Hobbes was the ancestor of a realistic or " hard " variety,
while Jean Jacques Rousseau, in the next century, began a different version which is romantic or " soft." [1]

Since this second kind of scientism concentrates on human
nature, it can be distinguished from the first by being described
as " psychological." Psychology, however, does not make its
appearance as a science, any more than sociology, until the
nineteenth century. Neither Hobbes nor Rousseau was a scientist, although their naturalism clearly presupposes the whole

73

" scientific " frame of reference of modern thought. Sigmund Freud was the first great scientific psychologist. Unfortunately, however, like his older contemporary, Karl Marx, Freud was not only a genuine scientist, who applied the scientific method to the study of man with important and far-reaching results, but he was also a scientolator, who made the same mistake about the possibilities of science in regard to human nature as did Marx in regard to human society — with the same potentially disastrous results. For the Freudian theories, as their author appeared at times to realize, also can lead in the direction of totalitarianism, and to a totalitarianism of the altogether vicious Nazi type.

The application of the dogmas of scientism to the human situation, whether to human society or to the human psyche, inevitably deprives man of his specifically human status and makes him a fit candidate for the impersonal mass society.

## Hobbes and Hard Naturalism

Hobbes's system, as we have seen, was thoroughly materialistic and deterministic. When human nature is thought to be entirely accounted for in these terms, the result is a naturalistic psychology. Man's nature must be defined in terms of natural instinct and his behavior explained as the result of the natural operation of instinct. In Hobbes's account of man, the essence of the human being is regarded as the instinct for power, and everything that he does " naturally " is determined by the exercise of this instinct. The reality of the human spirit and of human freedom is denied.

Further, if Hobbes, because of his basic dogmas, has to give a naturalistic and deterministic account of human life, he is also compelled, for the same reason, to adopt a naturalistic and relativistic explanation of human values. If justice, goodness, and truth possessed a genuine reality which exercised a real power over the course of human life, then the dogmas of materialism and determinism would be destroyed. All values, therefore, must be either reduced to the level of nature, as Hobbes reduced the meaning of " good " so that it became synonymous with "power," or else described as the mere products of social organization, as Hobbes defined "right" and "true" in terms of the prescribed laws and beliefs of the state.

This is "hard" naturalism in the sense that man is here regarded as entirely motivated by irrational, aggressive, and self-seeking instincts. A purely psychological solution of the human problem, along the lines of natural self-expression, is ruled out, since human life, in its natural condition, is in a state of perpetual chaos. Hobbes's solution, therefore, was sociological and took the form of political absolutism. This is, in fact, the only realistic solution, once the problem has been analyzed in the categories of "hard" naturalism. The explosive and anarchic natural instincts have to be subdued by powerful controlling forces. But naturalism rejects the idea of universal and absolute values which had always provided this necessary control. Nothing remains that is capable of playing this essential part except the absolute state and its inexorable laws.

Naturalism, like materialism, thus prepares clients for totalitarianism, but for totalitarianism of a different type. The roots of the difference can be traced back to Rousseau, who was born thirty-three years after Hobbes died.

### Rousseau and Soft Naturalism

The eighteenth century Rousseau inaugurated the "soft" variety of naturalism, which turns up persistently in modern psychology alongside its brother of the sterner version. "Soft" naturalism continues to interpret man as essentially a set of instincts, but it regards these instincts as beneficent and, therefore, advocates their untrammeled expression and development. This view of life is sometimes called "romanticism."

The naturalistic dogma, to the effect that man is to be defined in terms of his instincts, is the psychological version of the materialistic bias which is characteristic of the general "scientific" climate of opinion. In so far as "soft" naturalism is based on this dogma it is clearly related to this way of thinking. Nevertheless, the relationship is somewhat ambiguous, for "soft" naturalism, in Rousseau and in romanticism in general, claimed to be in rebellion against science and all its works. The revolt against science, with which this line of development began, was prophetic of its final result, which was the Nazi reaction against all that is best in modern civilization. If this seems paradoxical, it should be remembered that scientism is never able to appreciate the real nature and meaning of genuine science.

The eighteenth century is called the Age of Reason or the Enlightenment. It was an age that glorified science, reason, technical progress, and logic. Rousseau revolted against the frigidity and artificiality of a technical civilization, and in his revolt, as is so often the case, went to the opposite extreme of glorifying the emotions, the feelings, and the instincts, at the expense of reason and logic. "A thinking man is a depraved animal," he said.[2] All the evils of life are due to the corruptions imposed on nature by a scientifically inspired civilization; therefore, "away with civilization, and back to nature; away with the science and reason of the civilized man and back to the instincts and emotions of the 'natural man.'" This is the way to happiness, fulfillment, and perfection of life. Rousseau tells us[3] that one day on the road to Vincennes the scales fell from off his eyes as they had from the eyes of Saint Paul on the road to Damascus. He saw in a flash how man had fallen from the felicity of his natural estate; how the blissful ignorance in which he had once lived, at peace with himself and with his fellows, had been broken by the rise of intellectual self-consciousness. Society then arose, and social conventions began to restrict and stifle all freedom of natural temperament and impulse. We must shatter the forms of civilized life and return to the state of nature. We must shake off the trammels of reason and return to the free self-expression of the natural man.

Hobbes, of course, also used the phrases "natural man" and "state of nature" and insisted that man's instincts are primary. This is the naturalistic dogma which he shares with Rousseau. But Hobbes was a hard naturalist and, recognizing that the natural instincts were not good, maintained that the state of nature, far from being peaceful and harmonious, was rather "red in tooth and claw." Rousseau, on the other hand, was a soft naturalist and supposed that the natural instincts are good in essence and beneficent in operation. "Man is naturally good, and only by institutions are men made bad." [4] In other words, natural man is good; this is the doctrine of original virtue characteristic of all soft naturalism and directly contrary to the doctrine of original sin, to which, at times, hard naturalism comes very close.

The goodness of natural man, according to Rousseau, is to be found in the natural instincts and endowments with which all men are born. There are two basic instincts, namely, self-love and sympathy, and two basic endowments, namely, freedom and equality. By self-love he probably meant the instinct of self-preservation, and by sympathy or "natural compassion" the gregarious instinct. Man is naturally good in the sense that these instincts and endowments, if unrestrained, operate automatically for the benefit of all, so that natural man is at peace with himself and with his fellows. In spite of his self-love and egotism, he is naturally fraternal and filled with brotherly love because of his instinct of sympathy. He is also free in the sense of being unrestricted by social conventions, independent of others, and uninhibited in the satisfaction of his appetites. Finally, men in the state of nature are all equal in the sense that all are equally endowed with self-love, sympathy, and freedom.

Civilization has corrupted all these characteristics: instead of being filled with brotherly love men are filled with suspicion and hate; instead of having liberty men suffer enslavement — "man is born free and everywhere he is in chains"; [5] instead of equality inequalities of all kinds abound on every side. These perversions are due to the institutions of a culture and a society that have been built up on the basis of science and reason. The solution, said Rousseau, is to cast off the artificial conventions of society, to abandon reason and let the natural instincts and endowments express themselves without restraint.

This is the Rousseau that appeared in the earlier works, such as the *Discourse on the Arts and Sciences* and the *Discourse on the Origins of Inequality.*[6] Here both the analysis and the solution of the human problem were given in terms of a soft naturalism. The human problem, of course, is the existence of evil. According to Rousseau, evil is due to the fact that the naturally good instincts of man have been inhibited and perverted by the unnatural constraints of society. The way to salvation, at first, seems simple: abolish all inhibitions and let your nature express itself freely; the result, it is confidently expected, will be peace, brotherhood, and good will. The same analysis and the same solution of the human problem are still being given by the contemporary self-expression school of psychology which maintains the tradition of soft and sentimental naturalism.

In his earlier works, then, Rousseau proposed a purely psychological solution. Later, however, in *The Social Contract,* he came to see that the psychological solution by itself is inadequate, and consequently he abandoned it in favor of a sociological solution that, as it will become clear, was strongly suggestive of Nazi totalitarianism. This change in Rousseau's thought is characteristic of the development that takes place in the history of soft naturalism in general.

By the time that Rousseau came to write *The Social Contract,* he saw that some form of social organization is necessary for man. Even if it means the loss of the natural right of unrestrained exercise of instincts and of free enjoyment of natural endowments, some kind of society is necessary to provide mutual protection and security. There can be no question now of any return to a primitive state of nature. The choice is not between society and nature, but between a bad society (and all those that have hitherto existed are so regarded) and the good society, the principles of which Rousseau proceeded to outline. Instead of corrupting man's nature, the good society will bring it to fulfillment and therefore might be called a *natural* society.

The natural and good society is based on an agreement or contract into which all its members enter at the outset. In this contract each individual gives up all natural right to the free expression of his instincts and endowments. Its clauses, wrote Rousseau, " may be reduced to one — the total alienation of each associate, together with all his rights, to the whole community." [7] This is the price that he pays in return for the support and protection of the community. In case this should seem too high a price, Rousseau hastened to add that the individual, in return for the alienation of his *natural* rights, receives back *civil* rights which are actually of a higher type. In return for his natural freedom, he receives civil liberty; for natural equality, equality before the law; for sympathy, fraternity; and for self-love, patriotism. What these various civil rights actually meant for Rousseau will become clear in a moment.

The old natural rights must be given up to what Rousseau called the sovereign power. The sovereign power in the state is that part of the body politic in which the absolute and final power resides. In the good society the sovereign power resides in the people as a whole, and therefore it is necessary to distinguish between it and the Government, which is a small group representative of the people and to which they delegate enough power for the execution of their will. The will of the people which the Government exists to carry out is called the " general will." For just as the community as a whole is regarded as an entity transcending all its members and is called, on analogy with a living organism, the body politic, so this body politic is thought of, on analogy with the human body, as animated by a will. Now this mystical general will which drives the mystical body politic " tends always and everywhere to the preservation and welfare of the whole and of every part." [8] In other words, the general will is infallible. Rousseau argued for its infallibility in the following way: all the individual wills, being guided by self-interest, are different and opposing, and therefore automatically cancel each other out; what remains is the general will, which is common to all and therefore makes no mistakes. " The general will is always right." [9] This infallible general will is the source of all laws, which are therefore likewise always right, final, and absolute.

The general will, which is expressed and executed in the laws of the state, is the real will of everyone in the state because it always works out in the best interests of all. Now the definition of freedom is the ability to carry out one's will. Since the general will is the real will of all, and since it is carried out in the laws, then real freedom consists in obedience to the laws. This is what is meant by the " civil liberty " which all receive in return for their natural freedom. The peculiar character of this kind of liberty is seen in Rousseau's famous remark, the sinister implications of which it has been left to the twentieth century to develop to the full: " Whosoever refuses to obey the general will shall be compelled to do so by the whole body. This means nothing less than that he shall be forced to be free." [10] Further, since the laws of the state, which put the general will into practice, are compulsory for all without regard to birth, position, or ability, then all are equal before the law and have the same rights under the law. This is what is meant by civil " equality," which is received in return for natural equality. In the next place, membership in the mystical body politic and participation in the mystical general will produce a mystical feeling of fraternity or corporate solidarity in all who belong to the community. This is what is meant by " fraternity," which is received in exchange for the natural sympathy or gregariousness surrendered in the contract.

It is the state, formed by the contract, which replaces the old instinctive independence, equality, and sympathy with the distinctively human values of liberty, equality before the law, and fraternity. It is the state that gives man his human rights, making his behavior moral rather than instinctive, and turning an animal into a man. " Substituting justice for instinct in his conduct, and giving his actions the morality they had formerly lacked . . . [the good society] makes him instead of a stupid animal . . . an intelligent being and a man." [11] Thus, it now turns out, we can become men in the full sense only by becoming citizens, that is, members of the state. We therefore owe everything to the state, and it is for this reason that loyalty to the state, or patriotism, is, according to Rousseau, the highest virtue. Patriotism, being self-love writ large and rendered energetic, heroic, and virtuous, is that which all receive back in return for the natural self-love which was surrendered in the contract. This is the greatest and most glorious gift that society bestows on her children. "It is certain that the greatest miracles of virtue have been produced by patriotism: this fine and living feeling which gives to the force of self-love all the beauty of virtue, lends it an energy which . . . makes it the most heroic of all passions." [12]

Thus Rousseau who in the beginning had seemed to advocate the abolition of society and a return to nature now exalted his natural society as the great benefactor to which men owe their whole being. Life in such a society is far better and higher than life in a state of nature. For the natural society, far from corrupting man's instincts and endowments, is precisely that which, by giving him patriotism, corporate solidarity, civil liberty, and equality before the law in return for his natural self-love, sympathy, freedom, and equality, makes him a moral human being instead of an instinctive animal. This was Rousseau's justification for regarding the state, the body politic, the sovereign power as absolutely supreme over the individual. In doing so he was, of course, reacting against the trend toward individualism against which Marx was also to revolt. And Rousseau, like Marx, reacted to the opposite extremes of collectivism, saying, for instance, that men should become "accustomed to regard their individuality only in relation to the body of the state." [13] The eighteenth century exponents of the Enlightenment, like their nineteenth century successors, championed the individual and the rights of individual judgment and enterprise against the rights of the state, maintaining that the state existed only for the sake of individuals. Rousseau, on the other hand, like his successors, exalted the body politic and participation in the general will over against the individual and his private gratification, maintaining that the individual exists only for the sake of the state.

The totalitarian implications of this trend of thought are

clear. And that this development was inherent in the ideas of Rousseau is seen, first of all, in the history of the French Revolution, of which it has been said that *The Social Contract* was the handbook. The very motto of the new republic, " Liberty, Equality, Fraternity," was taken almost directly from that work. These are certainly the ideals of democracy, but the way in which Rousseau elaborated them meant that they could just as easily lead in an opposite direction. For the more the mystical body politic and its general will are exalted, the easier it becomes for one person or party to claim to be the sole authentic voice of that body and agent of that will. It was just this claim that the revolutionary government advanced when it achieved power in France. Robespierre, addressing the National Convention in 1794, said, " Our will is the general will "; and again: " They say that terrorism is the resort of a despotic government. . . . Yes, the government of the Republic is the despotism of liberty against tyranny." [14] Was it not Rousseau who talked of forcing men to be free, and is not this exactly the kind of " double talk " that is typical of contemporary forms of totalitarianism? The Party is the people; the suppression of individual liberty and natural rights is the only way in which to secure real freedom and self-fulfillment; dictatorship is really the highest form of democracy.

Hitler and the Nazi party made the same use of Rousseau's ideas in the twentieth century as did Robespierre and the Revolutionary party in the eighteenth century: " Our will is the general will; our voice is the voice of the people; if anyone resist us he resists the German people and must be compelled to conform." Nazism stemmed from many sources, but it is certain that it derived much of its political, as well as its psychological, inspiration from Rousseau and from the romanticism which developed out of his teaching. It is Rousseau's conception and glorification of the body politic that was aped by the Nazis. The state is a mystical entity, supreme over all and in relation to which alone all individuals have status and being. The doctrine of the general will leads in the same direction. The general will, because of its generality, is infallible, and as such is the source of infallible laws which, therefore, must be obeyed by all without question. In practice this means that the strong man who asserts the identity of his will with the general will is able to claim infallibility for his words and for his laws.

Again, Rousseau's conception of fraternity, as the civil transformation of natural sympathy, was taken over by the Nazis in their doctrine of the racial solidarity of the German *Volk*. For Rousseau fraternity is that which binds together all the members of the state in a mystical unity. For the Nazis, similarly, the *Volk* was mystically united by a common "blood and soil." The highest element in men is their common "blood consciousness" rather than their reason. Compare the Nazi "What we need is men who think with their blood" and Goering's "When I hear the word culture, I reach for my revolver" with Rousseau's "A thinking man is a depraved animal."

Finally, the Nazis followed Rousseau in glorifying patriotism as the highest of virtues. It might have been Hitler, rather than Rousseau, who described patriotism as "that most heroic of all passions." And we must remember that for Rousseau patriotism is simply self-love "writ large"; it is individual egotism changed into collective self-adulation, and thereby miraculously transformed into the most splendid of virtues. It is this kind of patriotism, accompanied by an emphasis on corporate solidarity, that becomes the source of all fanatical nationalism.

This way of thinking is indeed remote from science and even, it would seem, from scientism. Nevertheless, the influence of the "scientific" climate of opinion is apparent in Rousseau and in this whole line of development, in spite of the claim to be in revolt against the spirit of the age. The child who rebels against his parents is incapable of evading his background altogether and does not entirely forget the lessons that he learned at mother's knee.

Rousseau revolted against the artificiality and coldness of a scientifically inspired culture. These very characteristics which are fostered in society by the "scientific" tradition of life make a revolt against it inevitable. It is of the nature of science to be unemotional, and this is part of the secret of its success; but when society becomes " scientific," the consequent suppression or neglect of the whole affective side of life becomes intolerable. If the culture of man does not satisfy his emotional needs, he is likely to rush to the opposite extreme and surrender unconditionally to his natural feelings. "Science," said Irving Babbit, "thus actually prepares clients for the Rousseauist." [15] In fact, of course, it is not science but scientism that, by depriving men of any valid and controlled channels of emotional satisfaction, drives them into the excesses of sheer emotionalism. In this way, then, first of all, eighteenth century scientism was responsible, by way of the law of reverse action, for Rousseau's flight from reason to feeling and instinct.

The prevailing " scientific " tradition, however, not only lay behind the Rousseauist rebellion in this negative and indirect way, but also positively determined the character of the revolt. Rousseau might have attacked the predominance of science in the name of religion or of reason in some higher form; instead, he led the insurrection by raising the flag of nature. What was it but the materialistic bias of the " scientific " frame of reference which led him to assume that nature was the sole reality?

Again, Rousseau derived his conviction of the natural goodness of man from the same source. It was the very scientific progress to which he objected that made men ready to believe that they were capable of achieving the highest good simply by developing their natural endowments. The emphasis on human autonomy and self-sufficiency, characteristic of the prevailing tradition, prepared the way for Rousseau's doctrine that salvation and fulfillment were to be found in the expression of the natural instincts. It was the optimistic assumption of modern thought that gave him his dogma of original virtue.

Finally, the " scientific " tradition also made itself felt in Rousseau's political thought; for just as it affected his analysis of the human problem, it also determined the nature of his solution. Since nature is the only reality, it is there that man's salvation must be sought; if it cannot be found, as he at first imagined, in the individual gratification of instinct, then it must be discovered in the "natural" society. And the "natural" society, as outlined by Rousseau, already possesses the characteristics that were to be brought to their fruition by the Nazis.

## Hostility to Religion

It is evident that naturalism, like materialism, in so far as it accepts the dogmas of scientism, must reject not only the spirit and freedom of man and the universality of objective values, but also the reality of God, at any rate in the Christian sense. All these denials are implicit in the whole development of naturalism, but were not fully elaborated in theory until Freud began to write in the nineteenth century, nor rigorously put into practice until the Nazis began to act in the twentieth century.

Hobbes, as we have seen, was not an avowed atheist, but even allowed a place for the Christian Church in his ideal state; atheism, however, was logically entailed by his metaphysics. Similarly, Rousseau by no means denied the existence of God and even thought of himself as a religious man; but his religion was a kind of Deism, which was a characteristic eighteenth century attempt to reduce the essence of all religion to belief in God, immortality, and the soul; [16] and this, as Marx [17] was perceptive enough to realize, is simply "an easygoing way of getting rid of religion." It was really "nature" that Rousseau worshiped, just as it was "humanity" that was the object of devotion in Comte's "religion." But in the same way that the atheism which was implicit in Hobbes and already apparent in Comte had to wait upon Marx for its fullest expression, so the hostility toward the traditional idea of God which showed itself in both Hobbes and Rousseau only became quite forthright and unambiguous when Freud began to insist, with Marx, that religion was both false in its beliefs and pernicious in its effects. Both Marx and Freud regarded it as a perversion, but, in accordance with their different versions of scientism, the former explained it as a sociological phenomenon and the latter as psychological in its origin.

One of the first to formulate the psychological interpretation of religion, in the modern period, was Ludwig Feuerbach, an early nineteenth century philosopher to whom Marx was also much indebted. Feuerbach agreed with Comte that the influence of the Christian religion was now at an end, and that a new era in history, with new needs and interests, had begun. Modern man, he said, has abandoned faith in favor of science, has renounced the Bible and enthroned reason in its stead, has replaced religion by politics, put earth in place of heaven, material want in place of hell, and salvation through social reform in place of salvation through God.[18] It was in the use of this kind of language that he anticipated the Marxists, but his analysis of the nature of religion was psychological and was to be elaborated by the Freudians.

"Religion," wrote Feuerbach, " is the relation of man to his own nature — therein lies its truth . . . but to his own nature not recognized as his own, but regarded as another nature, separate, nay, contradistinguished from his own: herein lies its untruth . . ." [19] In this view, the concepts of religion are simply projections of elements in man's own nature, falsely objectified as attributes of a transcendent reality. From the nature of the human mind, we describe God as first cause (since the mind is thought of as the original source of its ideas), as self-subsistent (since the mind is regarded as independent of all else), and as one (since the mind is a unity). From the nature of the human will, we ascribe to God the moral qualities of goodness, justice, and freedom; and from the nature of human feeling, we assign to him the attributes of mercy, pity, love, and even suffering.[20] We must not make the mistake, however, of supposing that these religious ideas represent anything objectively real; they are simply the projection and idealization of our own characteristics and have only subjective significance. Their true function is not to signify a reality, but rather to stimulate us to the realization of the ideal possibilities within us.

In discharging this function, religion was still thought of by Feuerbach as playing a useful and important role in human life. Like Comte and Rousseau, he was anxious to retain it in some form. It remained for the later nineteenth century scientolators to take the tendencies of materialism and naturalism to their logical conclusion in hostile and aggressive atheism. It is impossible, of course, to stop with Feuerbach's alleged exposure of religion as a mere psychological illusion which nevertheless ought to be encouraged for its moral usefulness; religion is false in its beliefs but beneficial in its effects. The anomaly is obvious: religion could continue to exercise its beneficent power only as long as its ideas were mistakenly regarded as objectively true; the goodness of religion is dependent on a misconception of its real nature.[21] This divorce between what is good and what is true is intolerable; if religion is good, it is true, and if it is not true, it is not good. Freud was, therefore, much more consistent when he argued that religion is not only false in its claim to objective truth, but also dangerously unwholesome in its psychological operations.

The dogmas of scientism, whether in the materialistic or naturalistic version, cannot allow any place for transcendent reality any more than for the human spirit, human freedom, and human values. All these aspects of life and being belong together; either together they remain or together they go.

# 6

## Freudianism and the Nazi Society

•

SIGMUND FREUD, WHO LIVED
from 1856 to 1939, was as great a pioneer in the field of scientific psychology as Marx had been in the field of scientific sociology. Both these brilliant innovators rigorously applied the
principles and method of science to an area of reality that had
never been seriously investigated in this way — the area of human life. Marx applied the scientific method to human society,
and Freud to the human being himself. The conclusions at
which both arrived contained egregious errors, which were due
to a characteristic tendency to disregard the limitations of this
method and to make hasty and sweeping generalizations.
Nevertheless, the empirical evidence that they collected in
their respective fields and the hypotheses that they formed
with a kind of Copernican ingenuity opened the way to a much
deeper and more realistic understanding of man and his society than had been possible before their time.

Freud established the foundation of a psychology of " depth "
which is among the most important achievements of the modern era. Contemporary analytical psychology, while it has had
to correct its founder at many points, must always acknowledge its debt to the originality and genius of this first great scientific psychologist.

### Freudianism

With Freud, psychology broke away from the philosophical
context in which it had previously been set and explicitly
claimed to be a science, operating on the same principles as the

natural sciences. Freud always insisted that his theories were "conclusions which . . . represent the objective results of scientific investigation." [1]

What Freud, because of his scientism, would never admit was that when psychology became a science it gave up the attempt to understand man as a whole and, for the sake of greater accuracy, narrowed the field to those aspects of human nature with which the scientific method is capable of dealing. That method, as we have seen, is based on *limiting* principles which serve to isolate certain areas of reality. These abstracted areas can then be studied and analyzed with a thoroughness approaching completeness. The *genuine* scientist, of course, understands the nature of his procedure and never confuses the artificially isolated aspects of reality, which he is examining, with the whole of reality, which is, so to speak, too big for his microscope. Freud, then, without knowing it, was limited in his understanding of man by his determination to be strictly scientific.

He was limited, in the second place, by the fact that, as a doctor, he was dealing always with the psychically abnormal. It was his *patients* who furnished the initial evidence on which he built his theories about man.

Freud, of course, did not recognize either of these limitations as such. In regard to the first, he shared the general assumption of the age that the scientific method is the *only* reliable path to genuine knowledge. What science can discover about man, then, is all there is to know, and he could not agree that the psyche, as he described it, is not the whole man but only that part of man which science can see. As for the second limitation, he argued that all men are more or less neurotic and that the so-called abnormal is just an extreme case of the "normal." His theories, therefore, applied to man as such and not only to the mentally ill. [2] In other words, Freud made the typical pseudoscientific claim to have arrived at an understanding of the whole nature of man by means of the scientific method alone.

He began by designating "the pleasure-principle" as the

overruling law that governs human behavior. This principle he interpreted both materialistically and mechanistically: "We have decided to consider pleasure and pain in relation to the *quantity* of excitation present in the psychic life"; [3] "Our entire psychical activity . . . is *automatically* regulated by the pleasure-principle." [4]

Psychical activity, as in all forms of naturalism, is regarded as fundamentally instinctual. The instincts are distinguished into two groups, which Freud, at first, identified as the ego instincts and the sex instincts. The ego instincts are directed to self-preservation and find expression, for instance, in hunger. The sex instincts are directed to sexual gratification and find expression in what Freud called libido. *Libido* is simply the Latin word for "desire" or "appetite" or "lust" in general, but, for Freud, it is essentially related to the sex instincts as is hunger to the ego instincts. [5]

Both the ego and sex instincts are governed by the pleasure-principle, but the former have also to take into account the exigencies of external reality and thus to submit to "the reality-principle." They have to forfeit immediate pleasure and even endure pain in order to obtain the most pleasure in the long run; but since pleasure remains the ultimate object, the pleasure-principle is still in control. Similarly, while Freud did recognize, in a way in which his opponents do not always give him credit for, the existence of another set of instincts alongside the sexual, it is the latter that are all-powerful; for pleasure is the final end of life, and "the most intense pleasure of which man is capable [is] the pleasure in the performance of the sexual act." [6] Moreover, psychoanalysis went on to point out that the ego instincts "are also of a libidinous kind," [7] since self-preservation is a form of self-love or, in Freudian language, a libidinous attachment to the ego. Freud, at this stage, concluded that

"perhaps we have no other instincts at all than the libidinous ones. . . . In that event we must admit the critics to be in the right who from the first have suspected that psychoanalysis makes sexuality the explanation of everything. . . . It remains an awkward fact that analysis up to now has only put us in the position of demonstrating libidinous impulses." [8]

What is important here, however, for our purposes, is not so much the emphasis on sexuality as the strong assertion of the familiar naturalistic dogmas. The essence of man is his natural instincts, which determine everything that he thinks and does. Freud, as is normal in scientism, supposed that these were scientific conclusions, and did not understand that they were simply the inevitable result of assuming that the scientific method can give the whole truth about man.

The libido, of course, does not determine everything that we think and do in any conscious and direct manner. In order to explain the way in which the libido exercises its all-powerful influence, Freud introduced his second important hypothesis: the activities of the libido are, for the most part, unconscious. The conception of the unconscious, as the source of a large part of man's character, conduct, and beliefs, is perhaps Freud's most revolutionary contribution to man's understanding of himself. He pictured the psyche as an iceberg with only a small section of the total bulk above the surface; the rest is submerged, its existence unsuspected, but always active and potentially maleficent. Freud arrived at this conception by his observation of neurotic patients whose symptoms could be explained only by this hypothesis:

" It is undeniable that these symptoms . . . give the impression even to the patients themselves of being all-powerful visitants from another world. . . . In these symptoms lies the clearest indication of a special sphere of mental activity cut off from all the rest." [9]

The nature of the unconscious activities is decided very early in life. Soon after birth the libidinous tendencies of the sex instinct begin to make themselves felt. At once, however, the infant encounters obstacles to their gratification both from his own physical limitations and from the censures of parents and nurses. The desires are, therefore, " repressed " into the unconscious, where, nevertheless, they live and grow, always seeking expression. The psychical development which invariably ensues is the formation of what Freud called the " Oedipus complex ":

" At a very early age the little boy develops an object-cathexis [attachment] of libidinous desires for his mother; . . . as the sexual wishes in regard to the mother become more intense . . . the father is perceived as an obstacle to them; this gives rise to the Oedipus Complex. A wish arises to get rid of the father in order to take his place with the mother." [10]

When no satisfactory resolution of this state of affairs is achieved, the whole situation is " repressed," and the result is a neurosis in adult life. Normally, however, the adolescent succeeds in freeing himself from his desire for his mother by finding another love object, and from his hatred for his father by *identifying himself with him*. This identification with the father is of the greatest importance, because it is the origin of the moral conscience or, as Freud called it, " the censor." The prohibitions and taboos of society, which we call morality, and which had previously been external and mediated by the father, are now internalized and become the voice of conscience.

No one could deny that some such process may occur, especially in the case of patients in need of psychiatric treatment, but what are the grounds for supposing that it is the *normal* development of man as such? The answer is provided by the way in which Freud regularly generalized the clues which he discovered in clinical examinations. The connection between the normal and the abnormal is established by way of dreams:

" Since all men and not only neurotic persons have perverse, incestuous, and murderous dreams . . . we may infer that those who are normal today have also made the passage through the perversions . . . of the Oedipus Complex, and that this is the path of normal development." [11]

Freud's interpretation of dreams is the clue to his understanding of man's rational processes. Thus far everything that a man does has been explained by the unconscious drives of sexual libido. Does reason play no part at all in directing our thought and behavior? The answer is, " Very little." For Freud, "the ego represents what we call reason." [12] Now the ego, which is reason, is determined in its thoughts partly by unconscious libidinous desires, partly by the conscience or censor (which also owes its nature to the unconscious), and partly by the reality-principle, which alone bears witness to the external world and relates the ego to it. If the ego were always to act in accordance with the reality-principle, then all its acts would be strictly rational. But it seldom does. In relation to the unconscious, the ego (reason) "is like a man on horseback which has to hold in check the superior strength of the horse. . . . But often a rider, if he is not to be parted from his horse, is obliged to guide it where it wants to go." [13] The ego (reason) is "a poor creature," "a submissive slave who courts the love of his master," its master being, of course, the unconscious libido: "It draws the veil of its . . . rationalizations over . . . the demands of the libido." [14] The final conclusion is that unconscious and instinctive forces determine us to believe and to act in the way we do. "The conduct through life of what we call our ego [reason] is essentially passive and . . . we are 'lived' by unknown and uncontrollable forces." [15] And again, "Men are so slightly amenable to reasonable arguments, so completely are they ruled by their instinctual wishes." [16]

This is Freud's preliminary analysis of the human psyche, which is thus obviously neurotic and in need of cure. His proposed cure is the process of psychoanalysis itself. The problem is constituted by the fact that the repressed wishes of the libido become attached to unreal objects and much of the energy that would otherwise be at the disposal of the ego "is expended in maintaining the libido under repression and in warding off its attempts to assert itself. The task of the treatment, therefore, consists in the task of loosening the libido from its previous attachments . . . and making it again serviceable to the ego." [17] This is accomplished by tracing the process of repression back to its origin; the fictitious character of the objects of attachment is thus exposed. The libido is prevented from slipping back into its old ways, first of all, by being persuaded to at-

tach itself to the person of the physician; then " the new struggle which arises concerning this object is, by means of the ana-
lyst's suggestions, lifted to the surface . . . and is there worked
out as a normal mental conflict. . . . When the libido has been
detached from its temporary object in the person of the physician it cannot return to its earlier objects, but is now at the
disposal of the ego." [18] At the same time, the ego acquires a
" new capacity to expend a certain amount of the libido in
sublimations." [19]

So far we have been examining the way in which Freud handled the data collected in his scientific, clinical study of neurotic patients. Even here, as we have seen, he was unable to
refrain from generalizing his conclusions, in the typical fashion
of scientism, to apply to the whole of human nature. Elsewhere
he avowedly set out to construct what he called a " metapsychology," or theory of man and society at large. It is here that
we encounter the clearest formulation of psychological scientism.

To be complete, his metapsychology had to be set within
the framework of a metaphysics or theory of reality. For this
purpose, Freud simply borrowed the general materialistic-
mechanistic picture which was common in the latter part of
the nineteenth century. Dead, inorganic matter was postulated
as given. Out of this dead matter, life evolved by chance, and
this organic life eventually evolved into human life in the way
described by Darwin. It was at this point that Freud took up
the story and made his own novel contribution. The bundle of
living matter that is man is vitalized by an energy which proceeds from the " reservoir of the libido." [20] This energy joins
forces with the instincts, which were now grouped, not into sex
and ego instincts, since the latter have proved to be themselves
libidinous, but rather into " life and death instincts."

The life instincts are just the sexual instincts again, now subsumed, more politely, under the name of " eros." Their task, in
the whole scheme of things, is that of " complicating life by
bringing about a more and more far-reaching coalescence of
the particles into which living matter has been dispersed." [21]

The death instincts were given the general name of "*thanatos*"; their function is "to lead organic matter back into its inorganic state." [22] The representative of the death instincts is sadism, which, because it aims at injuring or destroying its object, cannot be derived from "the life-sustaining *eros*." Originally directed against the ego, it is "driven apart from the ego by the influence of the narcissistic libido, so that it becomes manifest only in reference to the object. It then enters the service of the sexual function," [23] which, therefore, remains, as before, supreme. The death instinct thus comes "to express itself . . . as an instinct of destruction directed against the external world and other organisms." [24]

Human life, then, in the Freudian view, is the scene of a struggle between life instincts, which aim at sexual gratification, and death instincts, which manifest themselves in acts of aggression. These are the irrational and inexorable forces that lie behind the mask of consciousness.

Freud's metapsychology not only produced this clear articulation of "hard" naturalism, but also systematized his earlier analysis of the psyche. The fundamental psychical reality, formerly called the unconscious, was now labeled the "id." The ego, or reason, is simply a modification of the id, due to the sense organs which give access to the external world. The third part of the psyche was now called the "superego" or "ego ideal" rather than the "censor," or conscience. Since its establishment is the way in which the Oedipus complex is normally overcome, and since the latter is rooted in the id, the superego stands, as Freud said, "as the representative of the internal world of the id." [25] At the same time, this rather unsavory character is also what we like to think of as "the higher moral and spiritual side of human nature." [26] Our so-called "higher nature," therefore, is in fact nothing but a "reaction-formation against the instinctual processes of the id." [27] Thus the id, with its blind pleasure-seeking instincts, is the real essence of the psyche; the ego is simply a modification of the id, and the superego is its "representative."

It is easy to see now what Freud meant when he said that

the ego or reason, in relation to the id, is a " poor creature " and a " submissive slave." Its only hope lies in increasing attention to the external world, and Freud eagerly grasped at this straw. But it is, after all, only a straw, for, according to Freud himself,[28] when the ego faces the external world, it simply finds another relentless master. For the reality to which the ego has access through sense perception is the materialistic-mechanistic universe, governed absolutely by the Newtonian laws of motion, and animated by living organisms the development of which is altogether determined externally by the Darwinian laws of the struggle for existence and internally by the Freudian laws of sex and aggression.

Freedom is a pathetic illusion. The ego is, in fact, enslaved to " three masters and consequently menaced by three several dangers; from the ' necessity ' of the external world, from the libido of the id, and from the severity of the superego." [29] Freud meant exactly what he said when he described his theory as " absolute psychic determinism " [30] and when he insisted that, as far as he was concerned, " determinism in the psychic realm is thus carried out uninterruptedly." [31]

## Freudian Atheism

According to Freud, the development of human culture, including its social and political institutions, its literature, philosophy, ethics, and religion, has followed the same lines, and is to be explained in the same way, as the psychical development of the individual: " The evolution of culture . . . [is] comparable to the normal growth of the individual to maturity." [32] This means that the impulses, repressions, substitute gratifications, and sublimations of the libido account not only for the course and character of the individual life but also for the whole shape and structure of civilization. Sexuality, indeed, explains everything.

It is quite evident that Freud simply substituted " sexual " for Marx's " economic " forces as the all-powerful determinants of human life and history. Marx regarded the economic influence as constituting an ideological taint which destroys the validity of all human claims to objective truth and justice and which perverts all moral, philosophical, and religious ideas into mere rationalizations of economic self-interest. In exactly the same way, Freud insisted that the repressed development of sexuality produces a neurotic taint which reduces the highest thoughts and most cherished convictions of the human race to rationalizations of sexual self-interest.

This " higher nature " both in the individual and in society is nothing but the content of the superego which, as we know, is established as a means of dealing with the Oedipus complex in the id. The social superego, like that of the individual, erects moral standards and insists with ruthless severity that all the members of the community conform. And just as the severity of the individual superego frequently produces individual neuroses, so the cultural superego is responsible for social neuroses.[33]

The fundamental neurosis of society, however, is religion. The hostility of scientism toward religion reached its climax in Freud, whose venomous attacks went to far greater extremes than the animadversions of Comte and Feuerbach and even surpassed those of Marx, and whose hatred seemed at times itself to verge on the pathological. " Religion," he wrote, " is the universal obsessional neurosis of humanity . . . a system of wish-illusions, incompatible with reality . . . neurotic survivals." [34] His explanation of the way in which it comes into being is well known. Like morality, of which it is the senior partner in psychical crime, it is the product of the resolution of the Oedipus complex. Belief in God as Father and Judge is a form of " father fixation." In childhood we have an exalted idea of our male parent's power and wisdom, and we are entirely dependent on him for protection. Eventually we are disillusioned in regard to his omnipotence and omniscience and deprived of his protection. But we still long for the ideal parent and finally project his image into the heavens as our Heavenly Father. At the same time, since the male parent is the author of the moral prohibitions, the source of threats and promises, and the executor of punishments and rewards, we make the Heavenly Father the giver and guarantor of the Commandments and the Judge who in the end will give to every man his due.

Religion, so understood, is neurotic in three ways. In the first place, it is an unhealthy " substitute for the longing for a father." Secondly, " the self-judgment which declares that the ego falls short of the ideal produces the sense of worthlessness " [35] or the " unconscious sense of guilt " [36] which spreads its blight over the whole of human life. Thirdly, " it invests the cultural prohibitions [of morality] with a quite peculiar solemnity " and by introducing the threat of divine punishment leads to psychical disaster.

This is Freud's analysis of human society; because of its moral and religious foundations, it is thoroughly rotten. What is the solution? Freud frequently appeared to be on the verge of suggesting, after the earlier Rousseau, that civilization must be abolished and that man must return to a state of nature. " It looks," he wrote, " as if our so-called civilization is to blame for a great part of our misery, and we should be much happier if we were to give it up and go back to primitive conditions." [37]

It was possible for Rousseau to make this suggestion because his analysis of human nature was " soft," and he evaluated the natural instincts as in themselves good. Freud, however, was precluded from this simple " back to nature " solution because his analysis was " hard," and he recognized the instincts as explosive and disruptive. If the restraints and prohibitions of civilization were to disappear, the state of nature to which men would return would be that which was described by Hobbes and not that which Rousseau envisaged.[38]

Freud's criticism of civilization, combined with his realistic view of the natural instincts, appears to have left him on the horns of a dilemma. On the one hand, the whole restraining structure of society, with its moral taboos and religious sanctions, is thoroughly neurotic, and therefore presumably should be abolished. But, on the other hand, " nature," which seems to be the only alternative, is chaotic and destructive, and if the prohibitions of society are removed, then the masses will return to the unbridled and fatal satisfaction of their instincts. For

Freud, there remained just two possibilities: "Either the most rigorous suppression of these dangerous masses and the most careful exclusion of all opportunities for mental awakening, or a fundamental revision of the relationship between culture and religion." [39] Freud, of course, preferred the latter alternative. It is not civilization but religion that we must abandon. A non-religious, scientific education, he hoped, would lead to a new kind of society which would be built up in accordance with psychoanalytical principles. The great social neurosis being cured and human nature being provided with a healthy cultural context, the danger of individual neuroses would disappear.

It seems strange that Freud pinned his hopes for the necessary social revolution on so negative a procedure as the eradication of religion. He thought that it would work out in the following ways: First, it would rid society of its worst obsessional neurosis; secondly, it would destroy the unwholesome sanctions which have grown up around morality; and thirdly, it would enable men "to admit honestly the purely human origin of all cultural laws and institutions," [40] and to understand, for the first time, the rational basis of moral prohibitions — namely, the need to secure peace and order in the face of the anarchy and war of nature. [41] In these various ways, the proposed non-religious education would lead to the triumph of the reason over "wish-illusions" and of the ego over the id and the super-ego.

The obvious difficulty in Freud's preferred solution of the human problem is this: If the reason is the "poor creature" and "submissive slave" which he had previously described, is it likely that it could be made master of the psyche in this comparatively simple way? Freud recognized the difficulty; he imagined someone objecting: "You admit on the one hand that man will not be guided by his intelligence; he is ruled by his passions and by the claims of his instincts; but on the other hand you propose to replace the affective basis of his allegiance to culture by a rational one." [42] Freud answered by simply re-stating his case: it is true that "men are [only] slightly amenable to reasonable arguments, so completely are they ruled by their instinctual wishes . . ."; but, he went on: "Have you asked yourself whether they need be so, whether their inmost nature necessitates it? . . . Think of the distressing contrast between the radiant intelligence of a healthy child and the feeble mentality of the average adult. . . . It is just religious upbringing which is largely to blame for this relative degeneration." [43] Abolish religion and remove the transcendental element from moral values, and then reason, by observing reality without prejudice, will bring mankind to the "psychological ideal, the primacy of the intellect." [44] This, in turn, will result in "the brotherhood of man and the reduction of suffering." [45]

Freud's great merit is to have described the human problem with the utmost realism and pessimism in terms of a psychology which is truly one of "depth" and along the lines of "hard" naturalism. The contradiction is all the more startling when it turns out that his solution is superficial and naïvely optimistic and belongs to the level of "soft" naturalism. It is, however, much more characteristic of the "scientific" age than Rousseau's recommendation that we should return to nature; Freud's hope is based on that blind faith in scientific reason as man's savior which can be explained only in terms of the optimistic temper of the prevailing "scientific" climate of opinion.

In Hobbes, both the analysis and the solution of the human problem were hard, the solution being totalitarianism. In Rousseau the analysis of human nature was soft, but, while in his earlier writings he seems also to have preferred a soft solution, in terms of free self-expression, ultimately he came to see the necessity of the hard alternative which is totalitarianism. Freud's analysis, on the other hand, was hard, while his preferred solution was soft. In the end, however, he too recognized the possible necessity of the same hard solution that both Hobbes and Rousseau had finally recommended. In some of his most striking passages he admitted, with typical honesty, that his optimism was possibly unfounded and his hopes merely illusions. "I know how difficult it is to avoid illusions; perhaps

even the hopes I have confessed to are of an illusory nature
. . . the optimism without foundation. . . . If experience
should show — not me, but to others after me who think as I
do — that we are mistaken, then we shall give up our expectations." [46] And again: " I will curb my ardor and admit the possibility that I too am chasing after an illusion. . . . But you
must admit that there is here the justification for a hope for
the future, that perhaps we may dig up a treasure that can
enrich culture, and that it is worth-while to make the experiment of a nonreligious education. Should it prove unsatisfac-
tory, I am ready to give up the reform and to return to the
earlier purely descriptive judgment: man is a creature of weak
intelligence who is governed by his instinctual wishes." [47]

The experiment of a nonreligious and nonmoral education
*was* tried in twentieth century Europe, but it proved to be not
so much " a treasure which could enrich culture " as the dread-
ful breeding ground of barbarians whose motto was, " When
we hear the word ' culture ' we reach for our revolvers." Others
after Freud, who thought as he did, came indeed to give up his
soft expectations and to have recourse, with catastrophic results, to what is, for naturalism, the only alternative possibility.
Listen to Freud himself as he describes the one solution that
will remain if his hopes turn out to be illusions and his followers are forced back to the " purely descriptive judgment":

" [Then] follows the necessity for . . . the most rigorous suppression of these dangerous masses and the most careful exclusion of all
opportunities for mental awakening. . . . [It then becomes obvious
that] it is . . . impossible to do without government of the masses
by a minority . . . who should be independent of the masses by
having at their disposal means of enforcing their authority . . . ;
and one may be appalled at the stupendous amount of force that
will be unavoidable if these intentions are to be carried out." [48]

Is this not suggestive of many passages in *Mein Kampf*, which
was to be written by another Austrian? Do we not hear already
the ominous tramp of marching feet in the night and the fear-
ful cries of the victims in the concentration camps? Freud himself was destined one day to hear these sounds. Did he recog-

nize them as the work of the evil spirit that he had helped to conjure up?

## Nazism

Why did Freud think that if his proposed revision of culture, based on science and reason, should fail, then the only alternative solution of the human problem was the " rigorous suppression of the masses "? And what is the justification for the suggestion that a Nazi form of totalitarianism is the outcome of naturalism? The answer to both questions is obvious, given the correctness of the following three positions: first, a hard naturalistic analysis of human nature as entirely determined by blind and brutal instincts; secondly, a relativistic ethics which denies the validity, and therefore the controlling power, of objective and universal norms of conduct; and thirdly, a naturalistic atheism which regards religion as a neurosis and the idea of an almighty and overruling God as the infantile projection of a father fixation. Hobbes, who advanced the first and second of these theses, quite logically proceeded to insist on the necessity of the absolute sovereign power of the state. For if there are no absolute moral standards whose authority men can recognize and submit to, their place can only be taken by the absolute laws of the state. Freud, who adopted all three positions, was naïve enough to suppose that the dictates of scientific reason might adequately replace the power of moral obligation and religion. At the same time, however, he was honest enough to recognize the possibility that such optimism was unfounded, and realistic enough to admit that if this turned out to be the case, then, as far as naturalism is concerned, Hobbes's authoritarian solution is the only one that remains. Since such naïveté and optimism are certainly illusory, it is clear enough for those who have eyes to see that a naturalistic psychology and a relativistic ethics may easily lead to absolutism in politics.

This conclusion is reinforced when, as in Freud, man's freedom and values are followed into the discard by God. In this case, not only are moral values replaced by arbitrary laws but Almighty God is succeeded by the Almighty State, which then begins to be worshiped with all the fanaticism of a false religion. Freud again foresaw this possibility when he put into the mouth of a hypothetical critic the following words:

"If you wish to expel religion from our European civilization, you can only do it through another system of doctrines, and from the outset this would take over all the psychological characteristics of religion, the same sanctity, rigidity, and intolerance, the same prohibition of thought in self-defense." [49]

Freud's only reply was a reassertion of his faith in scientific reason. As a matter of fact, Freud's hypothetical critic turned out to be a much better prophet than Freud; for it was the fanatical religion of Nazism that emerged precisely in that part of the world where naturalism had won the most numerous adherents.

It does not follow, of course, that Freud intended any such result; in fact, he was horrified by this denouement. Nor were the Nazis grateful for his help; actually he was forced to join the numerous band of refugees that his vicious progeny expelled from Europe. The irony of the situation is unconsciously illustrated by the words of A. A. Brill, in his introduction to a collection of the master's works: "Alas," he wrote in 1938, "as these pages are going to the printers we have been startled by the terrible news that . . . Professor Freud and his family are virtual prisoners in the hands of civilization's greatest scourge." [50] "Civilization's greatest scourge," however, had taken over many of its ideas from the man whom it then took prisoner. The Nazi ideology and political system, as the concrete historical culmination of naturalism, managed to combine the "back to nature" solution of the "soft" version with the totalitarianism of the "hard" variety. This was done in the first place by recognizing the natural instincts as chaotic and disruptive while at the same time evaluating them as "good"; discord and war are "higher" states of life than peace and harmony. Therefore, while the romantic and sentimental self-expression psychologists, who were the heirs of Rousseau, were prating of the sweetness and light to which the uninhibited expression of natural instinct would lead, the Nazis returned to nature as it really is; they put into practice the advice of these sentimentalists, with results that the latter did not foresee. The Nazis believed in the natural man, but understood him as he had been described by Hobbes and Freud, with his lust for power, sexuality, and aggressiveness.

The second way in which the Nazis combined self-expression and totalitarianism was by emphasizing the necessity of satisfying the natural instincts, not of the individual, but of *the race* as a whole. They understood that when individuals are allowed the unbridled gratification of instinct, the result is anarchy. This can be avoided, however, without sacrificing the principle of self-expression, by regarding the " self " that is to be expressed as the " self " of the German *Volk*, and the instincts that are to be satisfied as the racial instincts for power and mastery. In order that the gratification of these collective instincts might be secured, the German people had to be subjected to rigid discipline, regimentation, and absolute state control. Totalitarian methods were necessary, first of all, within the nation itself, in order to achieve the satisfaction of the German will to power. This in turn would lead to the imposition of totalitarian power to be exercised by the German race over the whole world.

Finally, Hobbes's lust for power and Freud's instinct of aggression were combined with Rousseau's self-love (transformed into fanatical patriotism) and fellow feeling (developed into exclusive racial solidarity). The goal of life was still conceived in naturalistic terms, but the individual expression of instincts was comprehended in the gratification of the racial or corporate instincts.

The Nazis simply applied and put into practice the theories of naturalistic or psychological scientism. Naturalism asserts that man is merely an animal determined in all that he thinks and does by unconscious and irrational instincts. The Nazis took this seriously and acted accordingly. The German people's lust for power was dictated by the imperious and inexorable voice of nature. Its satisfaction was the " manifest destiny " of the race. As the agent of its fulfillment, it threw up a " leader " who was guided at every step by natural intuition, and who, like an unconscious automaton, was "lived by unknown and uncontrollable forces."

"The sovereignty of necessity," writes Toynbee, "in the psychical sphere has also been proclaimed by one faction in our fledgling school of modern Western psychologists, who have been tempted to deny the existence of the soul — in the sense of personality or self-determining whole — in the excitement of an apparently initial success in an endeavor to analyze the soul's process of psychic behaviour. And, young though the science of psychoanalysis is, the worship of necessity in the medium of the soul-stuff can claim as its convert, in the hour of his brief triumph, the most notorious politician of the age. ' I go my way with the assurance of a somnambulist, the way which Providence has sent me.' These words are quoted from a speech of Adolf Hitler . . . and they sent a cold shudder through the frames of millions of European men and women beyond the frontiers of the Third Reich." [51]

In the next place, psychological scientism attacks the universality of moral norms, the validity of moral obligation, and the sense of moral failure; all ethical values are merely manmade conventions, which may have a utilitarian function in relation to social order, but which always exercise a traumatic effect in frustrating natural instinct. The Nazis eagerly adopted this position, and carried out its implications in the form of a wholesale attack on Western civilization and its traditional values. They rejected all moral restraints (were they not merely conventions?), and they gave their natural instincts a really uninhibited expression.

Under the leadership of the Nazis, the German people gratified their lust for power and instinct of aggression with no regard for generally accepted norms. Every conceivable kind of excess and barbarity was permissible, and in fact advisable, as long as it contributed to the mastery of the German race. This end and goal justified the slaughter of the Jews who threatened the purity and solidarity of the master race. It justified the enslavement of inferior peoples, the violation of solemn agreements, the abolition of the " sickly slave-morality " of Christianity, with its emasculating virtues of mercy, humility, and love, and the exaltation of the heroic ideals of self-assertion, racial pride, ruthlessness, and patriotism.

Both the similarities and the differences between the Nazi and the Communist " ethics " ought to be carefully noted. The similarities are due to the fact that both ideologies are forms of scientism which has encouraged modern man to reject all universal moral principles and to reduce all values to their pragmatic function. Both the Communists and the Nazis deny the validity of traditional Western morality and abuse the Christian ideal as, in the one case, a " bourgeois-" and, in the other, a " slave-morality." Both systems also regard the end as justifying the means. The important difference, however, has to do with the conception of the end. Communism aims at classless, equalitarian society, in which the brotherhood of man will be realized. Nazism, on the other hand, had as its goal simply the satisfaction of the racial lust for power, which would result in the world dominion of the German people. Finally, in Communist theory, totalitarian political arrangements are merely a means leading to the ideal stateless society, whereas in Nazism the totalitarian state is an end in itself.

Naturalism not only calls in question the reality of human freedom and the objectivity of human values, with the results that we have seen, but also goes on to undermine the validity of human reason; man is the irrational and helpless creature of impulse and feeling. The Nazis also took this doctrine seriously and put it into effect. Their creed was not expressed in rational terms, nor did it make any claim to objective truth (was not all " rationality " mere rationalization and wishful thinking?). The Nazi ideology took the form of open and unashamed mythology — the myths of " blood and soil," the Aryan race, the machinations of " world-Jewry," the infallible " Leader," and the " manifest destiny " of the *Volk*. No attempt was made to defend and propagate these myths by rational argument; the appeal was always to instinct and emotion, and the methods were the massed rally, the ceremonial parade, ritual chanting, frenzied oratory, and the whole gaudy paraphernalia of the Nazi regime.

The Nazi system was meant to give birth to Nietzsche's blond beasts and supermen. But while its children were certainly beasts, they appeared to be more submen than supermen. What totalitarianism in general produces are men who have lost their humanity. This abolition of man is common to both Communism and Nazism, but again takes different forms. In the one case, materialism is the underlying philosophy and economic forces the determining power; the product, on the human level, is the " economic man " — the cog in the economic machine. In the other case, naturalism is the metaphysical context and instinct the guiding principle; the end result, in terms of human beings, is the "faceless man" — the blind pulse in the racial blood stream.

In both cases, it is scientism that brings man to this end. Because of its materialistic and deterministic dogmas, it must regard man's spirit and freedom as illusions; it therefore deprives man of his dignity, of his integrity, of his special status in creation, and prepares him for extinction in the totalitarian state.

# 7

## Psychological Scientism

•

THE FACT THAT PSYCHOLOGICAL
scientism can easily lead to totalitarianism of the Nazi type is
itself a strong indictment of this way of thinking. It would not
be enough, however, by itself, to refute its fundamental dogmas, which might still constitute the truth, however distasteful,
about human nature.

What we aim to do here is to show, first, that these dogmas
are not, as they purport to be, genuine scientific conclusions,
but rather pseudoscientific consequences of uncritically accepted assumptions, and second, that they are also false to the
actual facts of human life. As in the case of Marx, however, we
have to be careful always to distinguish the important discoveries concerning the psyche, for which Freud as a scientist was
responsible, from the too hasty generalizations into which he
slipped as a scientolator. This distinction is made by many contemporary analytical psychologists, such as Karen Horney,
Gregory Zilboorg, and Erich Fromm, who are otherwise greatly
indebted to Freud.

### Criticism of Its Doctrines

Freud's root error was that of assuming that the *limiting*
principles of science are *universally valid* axioms. In other
words, he developed his system entirely within the context, not
of science, but of what we have called the " scientific " tradition
of thought. Instead of recognizing that the empirical method of
science restricted him to the study of those quasi-biological
aspects of human nature which are quantitative in essence and

determined in behavior, he supposed that science alone gives truth and that, therefore, human life can be fully explained in these terms.

The first dogma, then, of Freudian scientism, is the claim that what it discovers about man is the whole and final truth. Such an assertion is all the more surprising because the scientist in Freud knows that it is unscientific. " We must hold ourselves," he said, " in readiness to abandon the path we have followed for a time, if it should seem to lead to no good result. Only such ' true believers ' as expect from science a substitute for the creed they have relinquished will take it amiss if the investigator develops his views further or even transforms them." [1] This is one of the few warnings against turning science into a religion that is to be found in the literature of scientism. Unfortunately, however, Freud himself did not by any means always heed it. " Science," he wrote in another place, " is no illusion. But it would be an illusion to suppose that we could get elsewhere what it cannot give us." [2] Science is the sole source of truth and salvation.

If it is an illusion to suppose that we can get elsewhere what science cannot give us, then the future indeed looks black. For the knowledge and power that science yields is quite able to destroy both the human person and the human community, as long as it is uncontrolled by any higher wisdom. But surely it is absurd to suggest, especially in regard to human nature, that the accumulated wisdom of the world's great literature, philosophy, and religion is without any value. In fact, of course, their understanding and insights penetrate and illumine the depths of man's being to a degree that makes the findings of even " depth " psychology look superficial and two-dimensional. If man's story is not to come to a bad end, we must combine our scientific knowledge of the psyche with the deeper wisdom of the spirit.

Such collaboration between the scientific knowledge of psychology and the richer insights of the humanities would preclude the pretentious error of scientism which mistakes the scientifically defined psyche for the full human spirit. The scientist, looking at man through his peculiar spectacles, one lens of which is the quantitative principle and the other the mechanical, observes man as a biological mechanism and nothing more. *As a scientist* he is necessarily blind to the realities of the spirit; for the investigator can discover in his field only those aspects with which his method is capable of dealing. The genuine scientists conclude that this is man *as science sees him.* The pseudo scientist or scientolator insists that this is man *in his entirety.* But thus to force man into the limitations prescribed by a certain method of investigation is a Procrustean procedure, and the result is that the central question about human nature — what *is* man — is decided in advance of all impartial consideration.

Freud not only thought that science alone gives truth, but constantly wrote as if the truth that his science discovered was the absolute and final truth. This is the case, for instance, in his unqualified assertion that *all* neuroses have a sexual origin. For example, after discussing two particular cases, he went on to say: " Well now, what we have found in these two examples we should find *in every case* we submitted to analysis. *Every time* we should be led by analysis to the sexual experiences and desires of the patients, and *every time* we should have to affirm that the symptoms served the same purpose." [3] What is the evidence for this all-inclusive generalization which admits of absolutely no exceptions whatever? The evidence is simply that in all neurotic cases that had come under his care *his own explanation* of the sexual origin of the disease had been accepted by the patient.[4] In other words, the alleged " evidence " is nothing but Freud's own hypothesis or theory which then became regarded by him as a clinically discovered fact and was made the basis of a dogmatic generalization. But even if the evidence were genuine, he could not have known, in advance, that no exceptions to the rule would ever turn up in the future. The way in which he " knew " this constituted another departure from real empiricism. For in order to guarantee the universal validity of the sexual explanation, he *stipulated* that no other explanation must ever be accepted by psychoanalysis.

Whenever a neurotic refused to acknowledge the correctness of the sexual diagnosis, Freud determined, *in advance of investigation,* to regard this refusal as simply a " resistance " to such a shameful confession and as therefore actually affording further evidence for the truth of the theory. This highhanded procedure meant that the possibility of negative cases was ruled out, a priori; and this is a radical violation of the genuine scientific method.

Freud established his dogmas, first of all, by transforming his hypothetical explanations into " facts," and then by employing these " facts " surreptitiously as though they were genuine empirical evidence for his generalizations. He then went on to make these generalizations absolutely unexceptional ( which is one way of defining a dogma ) by ascribing all apparently contradictory evidence to the " resistance " of the patients who were unwilling to admit the sexual origin of their complaints and who thereby tacitly confirmed the correctness of the diagnosis. Thus all evidence, whether negative or not, was forced by stipulation to strengthen the theory. This procedure is a good example of what is meant by the term " unscientific."

Freud was equally dogmatic, of course, in insisting that man's *whole* being can be *completely* explained in terms of natural instincts which automatically pursue a quantitatively measurable pleasure. Some such naturalistically conceived psyche is undoubtedly an important factor in the human being as science sees him. To assert, however, that it is the real essence of man is not to enunciate a scientific theory but rather to declare one's allegiance to the materialistic dogma. This dogma, as we have seen, is so far-fetched that it can be explained only as the transformation of the uncritically accepted materialistic assumption of a " scientific " age, which in turn is simply a misreading of the quantitative principle of the scientific method.

The mistake of supposing that the quasi-biological psyche is the real man can easily be avoided, without sacrificing any of Freud's genuine insights, by regarding the Freudian psyche, in accordance with Dr. Zilboorg's suggestion,[5] as an " organ " of, and not as a " psychoanalytical substitute " for, the human spirit, and by understanding the term "psychological" to mean "the functioning of the psychic apparatus" and not as synonymous with "spiritual." [6] It is the failure to make this distinction that turns the Freudian system, and much modern psychology, into a form of scientism.

Pseudoscientific psychology, because of its underlying dogmas, has to treat all apparently nonnaturalistic factors in human life either by reducing them to the naturalistic level or by explaining them away. The first such problem is the nature of human thought which does not appear to be fully explicable in naturalistic terms. Freud attempted to explain it as nothing but a modification of the unconscious and instinctual id — "that part of the id which has been modified by the direct influence of the external world." [7] This attempt to reduce reason and consciousness, which make up the ego, to the level of the natural instincts, which make up the id, by calling the former merely a "modification" or "part" of the latter, is comparable to Marx's efforts to reduce mind to matter by calling the one a "reflection" or "part" of the other. And as in the case of Marx, we have to point out, first, that to suppose that human reason has been naturalistically explained simply by being *called* a "modification" of the id is to commit the nominalistic fallacy; we are still left with the question: What is the nature of this "modification"? Is it the same in essence as the id, or is it something quite different? If it is argued that it is the same on the grounds that it emerges out of the id, then it is the genetic fallacy that we are being offered; the argument is fallacious because the final product of an evolutionary development is not identical with its first beginnings. In this case the "modification" can be shown to be something quite different. Since the reason, with Freud's help, can come to *know* the id, it must transcend the latter in a way that cannot be fully explained in naturalistic terms.

If reason is "explained" in the Freudian system by being reduced to the level of nature, the second great problem for naturalism is "explained" by being explained away: the universal human conviction of freedom is nothing but an illusion;

"determinism in the psychic realm is carried out uninterruptedly." On occasion, however, Freud appeared to contradict himself by suggesting that psychoanalysis could confer a kind of freedom upon the ego: "Analysis," he said, "sets out . . . to give the patient's ego freedom to choose." [8] The contradiction, which is often encountered, of a deterministic psychology declaring that it can make men free, can only be resolved by admitting, as Freud would not, that the psyche which science knows is not identical with the human spirit. If, following Dr. Zilboorg, we think of the psyche as an instrument of the spirit, and not as its substitute, then, as he says, "the misconceived controversy about psychoanalysis and freewill will easily recede." [9] The materialistic dogma, however, will not admit of such distinctions, and psychological scientism is therefore committed to "absolute psychic determinism."

The essential paradox of absolute determinism is that if it were true its truth could never have been discovered. It would be impossible for anyone to rise superior to the determined order and to describe it in terms of an objective theory that was not itself determined by the unexceptional psychical mechanisms. What we must ask Freud and all other determinists is this: What is the vantage point from which you are able to give us this all-embracing theory of human action and belief? What position are you occupying that enables you to talk about absolutes, even "absolute" determinism? Is it not the case that this position is one of transcendence, in the sense that any being who can talk about the *whole* determined order of things thereby proves that he transcends that order and, in this respect, is free? Absolute determinism is thus self-refuting.

Absolute determinism means not only that all human acts but also all human beliefs are determined by forces beyond man's control and, therefore, cannot claim objective truth. I may imagine that I have decided to accept certain ideas because they are true, but this is an illusion; I cherish my beliefs, not because of their truth, but because of the demands of "unknown and uncontrollable forces" which are, at root, sexual in nature. In other words, there arises out of Freud's pansexual determinism an assertion of an omnipresent sexual taint in human thinking, which is parallel, point for point, with Marx's insistence, stemming from his paneconomic determinism, on an economic ideological taint. Both Marx and Freud accepted the dogma of determinism; they regarded it as " scientific," though actually it is simply a transformation of the mechanistic assumption of the general " scientific " climate of opinion, which in this case is due to a misreading of the mechanical principle of the scientific method.

It is scarcely too much to say that Hobbes, Marx, and Freud all believed in the doctrine of original sin: there is something radically wrong with human nature which distorts man's value judgments, tempts him to mistake his relative truth for absolute truth, and vitiates his whole culture. The curious fact is that each of these determinists singled out some one source of human evil, to the exclusion of all others, and attempted to make it the exhaustive explanation of human thought and behavior. Hobbes chose the lust for power, Marx economic self-interest, and Freud the repressed drives of the libido. " Every philosopher," writes Ernst Cassirer,[10]

" believes that he has found the mainspring and master faculty. . . . But as to the character of the master faculty all the explanations differ widely from, and contradict, one another. Each individual thinker gives us his own picture of human nature. . . . But their interpretation of the empirical evidence contains from the outset an arbitrary assumption — and this arbitrariness becomes more and more obvious as the theory proceeds and takes on a more elaborate and sophisticated aspect. Nietzsche [following Hobbes] proclaims the will to power, Freud signalizes the sexual instinct, Marx enthrones the economic instinct. Each theory becomes a Procrustean bed on which the empirical facts are stretched to fit a preconceived pattern."

The fact that the three factors chosen as the cause of the misdirection of life have something in common suggests that there is something underlying them all that is the ultimate source of human corruption. The various choices are all forms of self-interest; and perhaps it is this that lies behind the lust for power, economic greed, and sexual selfishness. If this is so, then none of them can be altogether overcome in isolation from the others and unless the source of all three is attacked.

We can agree that self-interest is powerful in determining our dearest beliefs, and that therefore their claim to objective truth must, in every case, be carefully scrutinized. But we cannot admit that, because of this, any claim to genuine truth is impossible. This absolute irrationalism, which is involved in the dogmas of psychological scientism and which the Nazis so eagerly embraced, is even more obviously self-refuting than the determinism from which it springs. Again we have some questions to put to Freud: When you make the statement that objective truth is impossible, do you not wish *this statement*, at least, to be regarded as objectively true? On the other hand, if your theory of absolute determinism refutes the objective truth of all beliefs, how do your own theories escape a similar refutation?

Freud's irrationalism is one example of his relativism in regard to values in general. The traditional human conviction that there are eternal and universal values of which man is aware is a third " illusion," along with the notions of spirit and freedom, of which naturalism, like materialism, has to dispose. " I . . . am sure," said Freud, ". . . that the judgments of value made by mankind are immediately determined by their desires for happiness, in other words that those judgments are attempts to prop up their illusions with arguments." [11] All moral standards, for instance, are really just conventional agreements, the *raison d'être* of which is to act as restraints on natural instinct, and the function of which is to preserve peace and order; peace and order, in turn, are essential to the greatest pleasure in the long run.

In this way, Freud reduced the meaning of moral values to natural meanings, very much in the fashion of English utilitarianism, which we shall have occasion presently to examine. [12] Freud's original contribution to ethical relativism was his explanation of the sense of obligation that binds us to our moral standards. If " right " simply means " useful," how does it happen that we think we *ought* to do what is " right," even when it does not appear to be expedient? This is a question that the utilitarians never satisfactorily answered. According to Freud, the feeling of obligation arises from identification with the father, which is the normal way of resolving the Oedipus complex, and which results in the setting up of the superego with its categorical imperative.

What Freud actually did was to give a description of the psychical mechanisms involved when we take over, as we undoubtedly do, the majority of our norms and standards from our parents and ultimately from our society. We have no quarrel either with the alleged social derivation of ethical principles nor with the description of the way in which the sense of obligation arises. But we do question the implications that, therefore, all moral values are entirely relative to a given social environment, and that moral obligation is neurotic. The first conclusion iş simply the familiar sociological relativism with which we have already dealt. The second is just one more case of the genetic fallacy; Freud supposed that an explanation of the way in which we arrive at steadfast allegiance to our moral principles is sufficient in itself to expose the hollowness of moral obligation; but a description of the psychical mechanisms by which we reach a certain state of mind has nothing to do with the general question of its validity.

As a matter of fact, Freud, like Marx and all other ethical relativists, firmly believed in the reality of certain moral values and in the obligation to pursue them. He spoke, for instance, of "the psychological ideal: the primacy of the intelligence." But to say that intelligence ought to come first in human life is to express both a moral obligation and also a judgment of value. He admitted the possibility that his *hope* that it might be *made* primary was illusory; but in his *judgment* that it *ought* to be, he never wavered. And, presumably, he did not consider that *this* judgment was an "attempt to prop up illusions with arguments." To judge from the writings of relativists themselves, it would seem to be a fact that the human mind is incapable of avoiding such judgments and the implied recognition of real, objective values.

The final dogma in Freudian scientism might be described as psychological utopianism. It is clearly a dogmatic articulation of the more or less unconscious optimistic assumption of the prevailing " scientific " tradition; and this assumption, in turn, is to be traced to a misunderstanding of the progressive principle of science.

In his analysis of the human situation, Freud produced a " hard," pessimistic account, in striking contrast to which was the " soft " and optimistic solution which he proposed. In the case of individuals, psychoanalysis, it was claimed, can make the ego master of the psyche by detaching the libido from fictitious objects and placing it at the disposal of the conscious reason. But what, we may ask, is to prevent the libido from returning once again to its earlier ways and thus producing another neurosis? Is the " poor creature " any better able than before to control its " masters "? This solution depends for its permanence on a miraculous regeneration of the ego, which the almost entirely negative process of psychoanalysis does nothing to effect.

Freud attempted to meet this difficulty by generalizing the psychoanalytical solution into a new type of education which would lead to a new kind of culture. This scientific education will teach the truth about human nature, in the form of the Freudian theory, and the truth about external nature, in the form of the Newtonian and Darwinian doctrines; and this truth will make men " free." A healthy civilization will speedily emerge, which will be liberated from the neurotic influence of religion and morality and which will be characterized, in Freud's words, by " the brotherhood of man and the reduction of suffering." [13]

An early version of scientism had hoped that the physical sciences would be sufficient to win salvation for men. Materialistic scientism saw that something else was needed, and pinned its faith on social science. Finally, naturalistic scientism, somewhat skeptical of sociology, suggested that the science of psychology is the key of knowledge which will open the door to human salvation. Freud put it this way: " One thought at first that the essence of culture lay in the conquest of nature for the means of supporting life [physical science], and in the eliminating of dangers that threaten culture by the suitable distribution of these among mankind [social science], but now the emphasis seems to have shifted away from the material plane on to the psychical [the science of psychology]." [14] Not only the physical but also the social sciences were now understood to be inadequate by themselves, and both alike were said to need the help of the master science of psychology. Freud criticized the purely sociological solution of Marx on the ground that "psychologically it is founded on an untenable illusion" [15] about human nature; he implied that sociology was worthless unless built upon the psychological foundations which he himself was willing to supply.

We can agree with this emphasis on the need for deeper insight into the nature of man and with these strictures on earlier forms of scientism. The question is whether Freud's psychological utopianism is on any firmer ground. The cultural revolution which he recommended consisted in little more than the somewhat paradoxical abolition of man's "higher nature." His new education, which was to be the agent of the transformation, was characterized chiefly by the omission of morality, philosophy, and religion which constituted what Freud himself called "the highest features of our civilization." [16] His attitude to these "higher mental activities" [17] was curiously ambivalent. He used these phrases to describe them, and at one point he said that "when they exist and especially when they are in the ascendant, they testify to a high level of civilization." [18] Nevertheless, in the end he recommended that they be suppressed and replaced — in the case of morality, by teaching the "rational" and utilitarian basis of cultural prohibitions, and in the case of philosophy and religion, by the teaching of science.

A further puzzling implication of Freud's solution of the human problem is this: Since morality and religion which belong to the superego are to be abolished and replaced by the rationality and science which the ego practices, it follows that the superego will cease to exist. This would certainly involve the death of the old man as described in Freud's analysis. For there the establishment of the superego was said to be the only way of resolving the Oedipus complex, which in turn was regarded as normal in man as such; and the entire process was said to take place in accordance with the laws of " absolute psychic determinism." Freud's new education, apparently, will interrupt this " absolute " process, and will produce a radically new man who will be free both of the Oedipus complex and of the superego. In other words, as in the case of Marx, where the appearance of the ideal society could only signify the end of the whole dialectical process, so in the case of Freud, the appearance of the new man would destroy the basic structure of the Freudian psyche.

### Criticism of Its Atheism

Adherence to the materialistic dogma entails a denial of the existence of God. The prior adoption of this dogma means that religious phenomena cannot be impartially examined, but must be studied only in order to be explained away.

Freud's explanation of religious belief is simply a translation into his own terminology of the familiar projection theory which was worked out by Feuerbach and which is standard in all forms of psychological scientism. Religious ideas are the objectification and idealization of certain subjective factors in human nature. In Freudian language, the idea of God is " a substitute for the longing for a father," a projection into the heavens of the image of the ideal male parent, an objectified " father fixation." Feuerbach thought that such illusory ideas served a useful moral purpose, but this position, as we saw, is too contradictory to be seriously maintained. Freud more consistently argued that wish-illusions are psychological maladies and must be cured.

In regard to this psychological theory of religion, we must, first of all, admit its basis in fact. Few theologians would deny that the attributes that we ascribe to God are formed, for the most part, on analogy with human qualities. In speaking of God we must begin from within our own experience; except for the *via negativa,* there is no other possibility. This means that the language that we employ in regard to God is always metaphorical. But the metaphorical nature of theological language, and its subjective basis, by no means weaken the probability of the existence of God. Indeed, if this objection were valid against the ideas of religion, it would tell as strongly against the ideas of science; for, as David Hume pointed out,[19] the basic scientific conception of cause and effect is derived from subjective experience. The fact that God is depicted in terms of idealized human qualities no more invalidates the reality of that which is so described than the subjective derivation of the idea of cause and effect disproves the uniformity of nature. As a matter of fact, if, instead of the materialistic presupposition, we begin with the assumption that man is made in the image of God, then the argument from the nature of man to the nature of God is perfectly sound.

The fact that God, in the Christian tradition, is thought of as Father was seized upon by Freud as evidence of the neurotic character of religion in general. Again we must first admit the degree of truth in the Freudian analysis. Let us imagine the case of John Smith. He is a deeply religious youth, with a vivid conviction that God is his Father. Eventually, however, he comes into contact with Freudian ideas which strike uncomfortably close to home. He realizes that the Freudian description of the way in which belief in God arises is perfectly correct *in his case.* He therefore abandons this belief. Then he proceeds to generalize from his own experience and arrives at the following conclusions: first, *all men* arrive at religious belief in the same way that he had; second, *all* belief in God is a form of father fixation; and third, *therefore,* there is no God. Now, up to the point at which John began to generalize, the process which he had undergone was clearly desirable. It was certainly necessary for him to abandon *his* belief in God which was nothing but a neurotic father fixation; he had been worshiping an image, that is to say, an idol. On the other hand, none of his conclusions is warranted on the basis of his experience. If he had refrained from this illegitimate line of argument and had, instead, begun to examine some of the perfectly valid reasons for believing in God, his last state would have been infinitely better than his first: and for this he would have had Freud to thank.

At the same time, it cannot be denied that Freud himself was guilty of the same mistake. Again he committed the genetic fallacy in the form of assuming that the psychological account of the genesis of a belief is sufficient to disprove its validity. A moment's reflection, however, reveals that the particular way in which I happen to arrive at a certain belief has nothing whatever to do with the theoretical question of its truth or falsity.[20] It may, of course, mean that the *psychological causes and motivation* of the belief, in my case, are unwholesome; but it does not mean either that this is true *in all cases* or, even if it were, that the *object* of the belief is thereby proved to be nonexistent.

It may be that the normal way in which we arrive at our idea of God is through the relationship with our male parent. This fact should not be disconcerting since we cannot arrive at any ideas apart from psychical mechanisms of some kind. Nor would it be surprising if it turned out, as Freud claimed, that this particular mechanism, like others, frequently gets out of gear and results in neuroses; as a matter of fact we know that this frequently happens; this was the kind of " religion " that Freud encountered in his patients and which led him characteristically to his antireligious generalizations. There is no reason, however, to suppose that the mechanism in question does not normally result in a perfectly wholesome belief in God, based on the metaphor of fatherhood. As far as the validity of this metaphor goes, we have the authority of One who, to say the least, was the nearest approach to " the psychological ideal " that the world has seen.

In comparison with this healthy attitude to God as Father, Freud's virulent hatred of religion appears decidedly neurotic. To say this is just to illustrate the Achilles' heel of psychological scientism in general, which is its defenselessness against its own methods of explanation. He who wants to " psychologize " the beliefs and attitudes of his fellows is always in danger of being "hoist with his own petard." If this method of "explaining away" is so universally applicable, it can be applied with equal force to the psychologizer and to the whole position on which he takes his stand.

The fact is, of course, that a respectable rational case can be made out both for theism and for atheism. The scientolator, however, is incapable of evaluating the strength of the theistic argument, for its truth would entail the collapse of his materialism, and this is a possibility that cannot for a moment be entertained. Religious belief *must* be explained away. He therefore fixes his attention on factors connected with the belief, such as its primitive beginnings or the subjective basis of its metaphorical expression or the psychological mechanism by which it is reached or the economic motives which sometimes lie behind its propagation, and arrives at the conclusions, respectively, of Hobbes, Feuerbach, Freud, and Marx. It cannot be repeated too often that whatever part these factors may play in religion, none of them has the slightest bearing on the question as to whether or not God exists.

## Psychology as the Key of Knowledge

All forms of scientism assume that the key of knowledge that will open the door to human salvation is to be found in science — either the natural sciences or the natural sciences under the guidance of sociology or the natural and social sciences building on the foundations provided by psychology. It has been suggested here that these hopes are all utopian and that the sociological and psychological versions in particular, if allowed free rein, actually lead to totalitarianism.

It may be objected that while Marxism and Freudianism may contain these implications, they are both extreme cases and do not fairly represent scientific sociology and psychology. The criticism is just, but care has been taken to distinguish what is scientific from what is pseudoscientific in these theories and it is the latter that has been attacked. Moreover, it is precisely as extreme cases of the danger of perverting science into scientism that Marx and Freud represent a widespread tendency in the contemporary social and psychological sciences.

It would be nonsense to suggest that sociology and psychology lead inevitably to totalitarianism of the Communist and Nazi types. The argument is, rather, that in so far as these inquiries claim to be strictly scientific, they are limited in their investigations to the quantitative and mechanical aspects of the human situation, and that where these limitations are misread as the whole truth about man and his society, the result is apt to be fatal to the human person and to the human community. An exclusively materialistic sociology, if pressed to its logical conclusions, tends in the direction of some kind of totalitarian economic collective, and an exclusively naturalistic psychology, in the same way, tends to move toward some form of totalitarian instinctual barbarism.

As far as psychology is concerned, its devotion to the scientific method commits it a priori to naturalistic and deterministic descriptions which it is apt to produce, with a great show of scientific objectivity, as the *results* of its investigations. If it fails to see that its naturalism and determinism are the inevitable result of applying the principles of science to the study of man, and imagines instead that they are all-embracing and scientifically proved facts, then it reaches the pseudoscientific conclusion that man is entirely a child of nature and altogether the creature of his natural instincts. The way to salvation will thereupon be envisaged either in terms of a return to nature as absolutely uninhibited self-expression or, when this proves intolerably anarchical, in terms of an authoritarian political system of the Nazi type.

The error is the apathetic fallacy which assumes that it is possible fully to understand man in the categories which are appropriate to the physical world. These categories, of course, *are* applicable to the human being in so far as he *is* a child of nature. The scientific method in psychology has therefore led to extremely important discoveries which we by no means intend to minimize. But if there are realities in human nature that are not found in nonhuman nature, then there is more in man than science can ever know. If there is something in the human being that may be called spirit, and if there is a real originating power that may be called freedom, then these aspects of human life simply remain beyond the scope of a strictly scientific psychology. It must not conclude that they are therefore illusions; where it does so, psychology ceases to be science and becomes scientism. Such a pseudoscientific psychology will not only fail to understand man, but by insisting on theories that are false to the real human situation may lead to disastrous consequences for the human person.

Psychology cannot be the key of knowledge that opens the door to human salvation. As science, it has a limited but indispensable role to play in the understanding of human nature. As a form of scientism, it can be used, as it has already once in Europe, to reinforce an ideology in which man, as a person, is abolished.

Scientism is the disease of the modern world, from which, as we shall see, the West has not remained uninfected. Communism and Nazism, springing respectively from the sociological and psychological varieties of the malady, are merely its most obvious and repulsive symptoms. The search for a cure of this illness need not, and should not, involve any derogation of science proper. Man's physical environment can best be understood, controlled, and improved by scientific methods. And in so far as man is himself a part of nature, his social organization and psychical apparatus can be handled in the same way and with the same beneficial results. If the social and psychological sciences, which understand this, were to recognize that man is also a free spirit, with heights and depths beyond their reach, and were to allow themselves to be subsumed within a larger interpretation of life, then, without ceasing to be sciences, they would take their rightful place and make their invaluable contributions to human welfare.

# III

•

## SCIENTISM, EMPIRICISM, and CAPITALISM

# 8

## Empiricism and Science

•

THE ANGLO-SAXON TYPE OF SCI-
entism is differentiated from the other two versions, first, in
being less dogmatic, and, second, in putting its faith in science
in general rather than in the social or psychological sciences in
particular.

This third variety of scientism finds its clearest expression in
empirical philosophy, which has been the main school of
thought in the democratic West. The very name "empiricism"
reveals the debt that this way of thinking owes to the "scientific" climate of opinion which has been the prevailing intellectual and social influence in the modern period. Empirical philosophy attempts to investigate all problems by means of the
empirical method of science which, as we have seen, is actually
restricted by its nature, and is so employed in science proper,
to certain areas of existence.

Empiricism, in philosophy, began to take shape in the sixteenth century writings of Francis Bacon, was carried farther
forward in the next century by John Locke, and arrived at
one of its two possible conclusions, which seemed to bring it
to a full stop, in the eighteenth century skepticism of David
Hume.

Empirical scientism is, for the most part, much more hypothetical and tentative in its conclusions than its more dogmatic
brothers, but at the same time it shares with them all the presuppositions and biases of the "scientific" age. It thus faces
two dangers. On the one hand, because of its disinclination to
be committed once and for all to any conclusion, it is likely to
degenerate into a paralyzing skepticism of the Humean type;

on the other hand, because of its assumptions, it is always in danger of hardening into something resembling the more extreme forms, to which, after all, it is closely related by descent and by common blood.

## Locke, Hume, and Skepticism

At the end of the sixteenth century, Francis Bacon was greatly impressed by the new method of inquiry which was already being employed so successfully in the natural sciences. In his *Novum Organum,* he recommended that philosophy and human thought in general should substitute this method for the older one. The only kind of knowledge, he said, that can be regarded as genuine is that which increases human power,[1] and it is the scientific method that alone leads to this result. If this method were universally applied, it would result in a veritable empire of mankind over the universe.[2] Here we see already the influence of the empiricistic and optimistic axioms of the " scientific " tradition of thought.

From a philosophical point of view, Bacon's wholehearted acceptance of the empirical method was quite uncritical. Before it could be adopted as the key to all problems, its credentials had to be more carefully examined. It was to this task that John Locke applied himself in the latter part of the seventeenth century.

Since the empirical method begins and ends with observation by the senses, the first question concerns the notorious unreliability of the senses: they are prone to illusions and to contradictory reports. How can real knowledge result from the information that they give? Locke attempted to meet the difficulties by analyzing the nature of sense perception. In perception, he said, there are three factors: the mind, the object, and the mind's idea of the object. What is directly present to the mind is never the object itself, but always an idea which *represents* the object; an idea is true when it *corresponds* to the thing that it represents. This representational theory of perception and this correspondence theory of truth were characteristic of empiricism until the nineteenth century.

Locke thought that this analysis enabled him to meet the difficulty of the unreliability of the senses. Some ideas represent real qualities in objects; these are the ideas of "primary qualities"—solidity, extension, motion, shape, and number (all *quantitative* characteristics). Other ideas appear to represent real qualities but actually do not; these are the ideas of "secondary qualities"—color, sound, taste, and so on. Secondary qualities do not belong to objects but only to our minds; they are the result of the impact on our sense organs of external objects with their real primary qualities. The unreliability of sense experience was thus explained in terms of secondary qualities. Our ideas of primary qualities, however, were said to be thoroughly trustworthy, and genuine knowledge of reality could be constructed on the basis of the information that they provided.[3]

Locke proceeded to build up this knowledge. We find, he said, that our simple ideas of primary qualities are regularly related to each other to form complex ideas. The most important of these are the ideas of substance and causality. First of all, when we find a number of ideas regularly occurring together in a group, we infer that they belong to the same thing. This thing to which qualities belong is the substance. The table is two feet long in size, and square in shape; but these qualities of size and shape must belong to something, namely, the table itself, and this "something," this thing itself, is the substance.[4] Secondly, when we find certain ideas repeatedly occurring in regular succession, we infer that the first is the cause of the second. Whenever wax melts we find that a flame is present. We therefore conclude that the flame causes the wax to melt, and thus we derive the complex idea of causality.[5]

Thus sense experience on the secondary level can be ruled out as illusory, but sense experience on the primary level gives us trustworthy information about external reality. This information reveals to us that external reality is made up of substances that possess real qualities of size, shape, number, and motion, and that are related to each other in real causal connections. Now this, of course, is precisely the picture of reality that seventeenth century science assumed. Locke thought that by his analysis of sense perception he had both justified this assumption and validated the empirical approach to reality.

Locke admitted that all this empirical "knowledge" is based on inference. From our ideas of primary qualities we infer that there are real qualities in things that are accurately represented by these ideas; and from the regularity of the coexistence and succession of our ideas we infer that substance and causality are realities in the external world. This kind of inferential "knowledge" is in fact, as Locke admits, just "faith or opinion." We simply have a "conviction," he said, that reality corresponds to our simple ideas of primary qualities and to our complex ideas of substance and causality.[6] Thus in the end we find that the whole empirical conception of reality is based on nothing but opinion and subjective conviction.

David Hume, in the next century, showed conclusively that the logical result of these tendencies is extreme skepticism. If we remain strictly empirical, refusing to indulge in hazardous inferences or to go beyond the reports of immediate sense impressions, we shall be unable to arrive at genuine knowledge of any kind.

It is true that certain sense impressions regularly occur in groups and we therefore say that they belong to "the same thing"; this "thing" is Locke's so-called substance. But all that we actually *observe* are impressions that happen to coexist. It is our minds, and not the given experiences, that contribute the idea of the substantial thing. If we are to be rigorously empirical, therefore, we can assert only the presence of coexisting impressions and not the existence of substances.[7]

Similarly, certain sets of impressions are found to succeed each other in a regular sequence and we say that the first is the cause of the second; this is the origin of the idea of causality. But again, all that we actually *observe* are sets of impressions which happen to succeed each other. It is our minds, and not the given experiences, that contribute the idea of invariable causal connections. If we are to be strictly empirical, we must content ourselves with asserting the occurrence of succession and say nothing about cause and effect.[8]

According to Hume, then, if empiricism is pressed to its logical conclusion, its two basic conceptions of substance and causality, which are also two of the fundamental assumptions of the "scientific" tradition of thought (the materialistic and mechanistic axioms), turn out, in fact, to be merely inventions of the human mind, with no possible empirical verification. Hume did point out that while we cannot regard these concepts as objectively true, we must admit that both for science and for everyday life they are useful fictions.[9] This clue was to be picked up later by pragmatism,[10] but, for Hume, it did not mitigate the conclusion that empiricism leads to skepticism in regard to the validity of scientific knowledge.

## Darwin and Empiricism

Empiricism, with its devotion to the scientific method, was theoretically annihilated by the analysis of Hume. This criticism, however, was academic and philosophical; it by no means signalized the end of the attempt of human reason to arrive at a comprehensive knowledge of reality in this way. For over against Hume's devastating theoretical attacks were the numerous and undeniable practical successes of science which were especially remarkable in the century after Hume. As a consequence of these successes, empirical scientism blossomed forth again with renewed self-confidence.

Perhaps the greatest contribution in this connection was made by Charles Darwin, yet another Englishman, who lived from 1809 to 1882. His theory of evolution, described in *The Origin of Species* (1859) and in *The Descent of Man* (1871), was one of the great successes of nineteenth century science, and it had the most far-reaching effects on philosophy and religion.

Darwin was not the first to entertain the idea of evolution, but he provided it with a firm foundation of empirical evidence, and put it in a form that made possible the prediction and assertion of a number of facts, the presence of which was confirmed by subsequent investigation. On the basis of a great variety of observations and experiments, carried out over a long period of time, Darwin formulated a hypothesis of the organic evolution of life in terms of "struggle for existence," "survival of the fittest," "heredity," "variations," and "natural selection." In each generation nature produces more organisms than are able to grow to maturity under the existing conditions of their environment. Hence the organisms struggle with each other for survival. Those organisms that are best adapted to the environment survive and reproduce, while the others perish. According to the laws of heredity, those characteristics of the surviving organisms, in virtue of which they were well adapted to their environment, are passed on to their offspring, enabling these in turn to survive and reproduce.

In spite of the fact that organisms pass on their favorable characteristics to their offspring, there are always differences between parents and descendants and between the descendants themselves. These differences or variations make their possessors either more or less well adapted to the environment. According to the principle of survival of the fittest, those offspring that are fortunate enough to acquire favorable variations are the ones that survive in the struggle for existence and that reproduce, passing on their acquired characteristics to their young in accordance with the law of heredity. Variations continue to accumulate in this way until a species is produced which is so entirely different from the original ancestral organism that it must be called a *new* species. The emergence of new species is thus the result of a process that operates entirely under natural laws and is called, in the theory, natural selection. The appearance of the radically distinct type of species known as man is to be explained in this way. He is entirely a product of natural forces and his lineage can be traced back through a long line of animal ancestors which have gradually evolved in accordance with natural selection.

The existence of man himself, with his distinctive intellectual and moral characteristics, had previously been regarded as evidence for a spiritual level of reality which lay beyond the scope of scientific investigation. Now, however, almost for the first time, we encounter the claim that science can explain these faculties as well. Darwin described the human intellect as simply an evolutionary development of animal intelligence, achieved through natural selection and hastened by the invention of language.[11] The moral faculty was similarly traced back to the gregarious instinct and the pleasure-principle in animals. Animal gregariousness is the source of the social instinct which, with its accompanying concern for public opinion and aided by the development of memory, is the essence of conscience. The pleasure-principle is the second source of morality: " as all wish for happiness [that is, pleasure], the ' greatest happiness principle ' will have become a most important secondary guide and object." [12]

The Anglo-Saxon Darwin here provided a " scientific " reduction of thought and morality of which Marx and Freud were to make good use. Indeed, Marx, as we have seen, applied the concept of evolution to the whole of reality. In any case, all forms of scientism eagerly embraced this theory, according to which man is an animal and only differs from the other animals in the number and degree of his variations. He is not marked off from the rest of nature by virtue of his spirit and freedom, but is purely animal in nature and altogether determined in behavior. Thus man was dethroned by Darwin from his special status in creation; he was on the way to becoming the Marxist or Freudian man who is a candidate for the mass society. Empirical scientism under the influence of Darwin began to harden into a more fatal mold.

## Hostility to Religion

Empiricism was saved from its logical conclusion in extreme skepticism by the practical successes of science. Nature was yielding up more and more of its secrets, and man himself had now been accounted for in scientific terms. But there remained a third area of human experience which surely remained beyond the reach of empirical investigations. Did not religion bear witness to a realm which transcended scientific knowledge?

John Locke did not think so. In fact, while remaining a sincere believer himself, he began the process by which the traditional religion of the West was gradually refined away and was replaced, at first by "natural" religion and finally by thoroughgoing agnosticism. Revelation, of course, was the first to go. Locke attempted to include it on condition that it present its empirical "testimonies and proofs." [13] He thought that Christianity fulfilled the condition in the shape of the miracles and prophecies recorded in the Bible and was therefore acceptable to empiricism.

Miracles and prophecies, of course, so far from being empirical evidence of revelation, are actually an affront to empirical reason. When this became obvious, revelation, which Locke had tied to miracles, was rejected along with them. The result was the eighteenth century "natural" religion, called Deism, which confined its creed to belief in God, the soul, and immortality. These doctrines, it was claimed, were not only the real essence of all religions but also capable of rational proof. Some Deists continued to regard themselves as Christians and were the forerunners of contemporary modernism. The more honest of them, however, understood that this was to water down the full Christian faith to an absurd degree and refused to call themselves by this name, while a few, identifying "God" with "the first cause," rejected the concept of spirit altogether and were frankly materialistic. Thus Deism, like empiricism in general, tended to develop in the direction either of complete skepticism or of dogmatic materialism.

It was Hume again who showed that the former is one inevitable conclusion of empiricism. The empirical method, if rigorously applied, demolishes both Locke's defense of Christianity and the Deistic "proofs" of religion. The alleged miracles, as evidence of revelation, cannot be accepted by empiricism. Even if we interpret cause and effect in terms of regular sequences, there is overwhelming empirical evidence for the uniformity of nature, in accordance with which for every event that happens in nature there is always a preceding natural event which we call its cause. In view of the great mass of evi-

dence that supports this hypothesis, any alleged exception to
the uniformity of nature would require a quite extraordinary
amount of indisputable evidence. The Biblical miracles are
such alleged exceptions. What is the evidence of their occurrence? It is nothing but the testimony of a few eyewitnesses.
Now, *against* the occurrence of miracles is the uniformity of
nature, which experience everywhere confirms, and in *support*
of them is merely the evidence of a few witnesses. Which is
more probable: that the uniformity of nature should be interrupted or that the reports of a few not impartial observers
should be mistaken? The answer is obviously the latter, for
experience teaches us not only that the uniformity of nature is
invariable, but also that the reports of eyewitnesses are often
confused, contradictory, and erroneous.[14]

Exactly the same type of argument can be used against the
alleged fulfillment of prophecy, which is really a kind of miracle. Thus the "testimonies and proofs" that Locke thought
validated the Christian revelation are discredited, and if we are
to remain strictly empirical the truth of revealed religion must
be rejected.

The alleged rational truths of natural religion or Deism are
on no firmer ground. The typical Deistic argument for the existence of God was Locke's causal argument. Every event has
a cause; and if we trace the series of events back far enough,
we must come to a first cause, since an infinite series of causes
is unthinkable. This first cause is God. Hume answered this
argument by recalling his own analysis of causation. The idea
of causation really stands for the relation between two events
which we repeatedly observe happening in regular sequence.
Now we do *not* repeatedly observe the universe and its history happening after some event that could be called its cause.
We are not entitled on the basis of empirical evidence to speak
of the universe as caused by anything whatever. Thus Hume
showed that empiricism, when relentlessly applied, forces natural as well as revealed religion into oblivion.[15]

Hume's religious skepticism, which was widespread in the
eighteenth century,[16] was eventually reinforced by the same

theory that helped to restore the prestige of scientific knowledge. The evolutionary hypothesis had antireligious implications which, while not drawn by Darwin himself, who for the
most part remained a genuine scientist, were quickly emphasized by Anglo-Saxon scientolators like T. H. Huxley.

In the first place, the Darwinian theory appeared to contradict the story of man's creation in Genesis, and thus to cast
doubt on the Biblical doctrine of man which taught that he was
made in the image of God. The intellectual and moral faculties
which were thought to support that doctrine were explained,
as we have seen, in naturalistic terms. In the second place, the
theory seemed to cut the ground from under at least one of
the traditional proofs of the existence of God. Before Darwin,
it was generally assumed that all the various species of things
were, and always had been, separate and distinct from one another. The origin of these fixed and multitudinous species could
be explained only by postulating a Creator who made each
with its own unchanging form. Further, the intricate and perfect adaptation enjoyed by creatures who were themselves
without intelligence seemed to point to a wise Providence who
endowed them with just the instincts and attributes that would
enable them to survive in their appointed environment. From
the evolutionary point of view, however, no purposeful creation is needed to explain these facts. Given the laws that this
theory formulated, it inevitably follows that the creatures that
survive are those with organs best adapted by nature to their
surroundings. Thus the evidence which supported the teleological argument for God received a scientific explanation.

Darwinism saved the Anglo-Saxon version of scientism from
skepticism and brought it into closer conformity to other varieties. It immensely strengthened the empiricistic, materialistic,
and optimistic axioms of the age. God is an unnecessary postulate; man is just a clever animal; evil is only a hangover from
our animal ancestry, and salvation is bound to come in the
course of further evolution assisted by scientific progress. When
conclusions of this kind were being stressed by certain pseudo
scientists as the necessary consequence of accepting evolution,

it is not surprising that some religious people put themselves in the false and dangerous position of maintaining that either evolution was wrong or else religion was false. When it was subsequently proved beyond much doubt that evolution was at any rate true in principle, there were many who concluded — and pseudo religion was as much to blame as pseudo science — that they must give up their faith.

The dilemma, however, was not genuine; for it is not the Darwinian theory itself that conflicts with true religion but only certain implications that were drawn by scientism. It is no longer possible to doubt the truth of evolution in general. What has to be denied is the claim that the theory necessarily has the destructive effect on religious belief which historically it seems to have exerted. The antireligious conclusions which have been drawn from Darwin's hypothesis may be questioned in two ways: first, the claim that the theory renders the postulate of God unnecessary is certainly invalid; for it makes no attempt to explain either the origin of matter or the emergence of life out of inorganic matter. Secondly, the idea that the hypothesis fully accounts for the nature of man is likewise untenable.

To take the latter point first, we have several times exposed the genetic fallacy that lies behind all such attempts at reduction. The end product of a long line of development cannot logically be identified with nor fully explained by its remote origins. Indeed, as far as ultimate explanations are concerned, it would seem to be much more plausible to argue that it is just the other way round: the first beginnings are to be explained finally in terms of their end results.

Lecomte du Noüy, in his *Human Destiny*,[17] deals effectively with the other point. He argues that if you abandon the notion of divine creation, then, in the first place, the existence of original inorganic matter remains a complete mystery, and, in the second place, the emergence of living matter out of dead matter has to be ascribed to chance. Putting aside the first question, for the moment, he calculates the chance collocation of the elements necessary to produce life. First of all, proteins are necessary; according to du Noüy's figures, the odds against the formation of *one* protein by chance alone are astronomical. Of course it is possible that by an extraordinary stroke of luck one protein was formed in this way. But life could not appear until many proteins had come together to make molecules. It is conceivable that by a kind of miracle of luck, two or three proteins were produced at the same time to make one molecule. But in order to make matter come alive, one molecule is of no use at all; hundreds of millions of molecules are necessary. If the appearance of one molecule was an extraordinary miracle, what are we to say of the simultaneous production of the millions of molecules necessary for the emergence of life? It could not have happened by chance alone. It must have been the result of what science itself sometimes calls " antichance," which, in more straightforward language, is known as purpose. In short, it must have been the act of a purposeful Creator and part of a teleological creation. If this is a necessary postulate, even for Darwinism, then we also have an explanation of the origin of matter itself, and we are back where we started.

It was not Darwin but scientism that set his theory in the pseudoscientific metaphysical framework; and it is the latter alone that has atheistic implications. Darwin, for his part, was content to give a scientific description of the emergence of the human species, and here he has much to say that is true and important. But when he suggested that his theory had fully explained the human being, he slipped, as Marx and Freud did, out of science and into scientism. His theory was true, but only true within limits and not the whole truth; that is to say, like all scientific hypotheses it was an abstraction, in the sense that it dealt with a more or less artificially isolated cross section of the total field. The spectacles through which it looked at the process that resulted in man were the spectacles of the scientific method. It could see, therefore, in this process only what its lenses permitted it to see. It could see natural causes, origins, and laws, but not reasons, ends, and purposes. And the ultimate explanation of the existence of matter, the emergence of life, and the appearance of man can be given only in terms of a creative purpose which lies behind the whole process and toward which, as its final goal, the course of evolution moves.

The only theory that fits all the facts is the teleological explanation which accounts for the lower in terms of the higher, the beginnings in terms of the ends, and finally describes the whole process in terms, so to speak, of a " pull from in front." This is the religious and personalistic explanation of all things; it does not contradict, but simply operates on a different level — looks through different spectacles — from the scientific account. Science is bound to mechanical causation, which explains the higher in terms of the lower, the later in terms of the earlier, and accounts for everything in terms of a " push from behind." This kind of explanation has its own very important place; it is only when it claims, by a kind of self-contradiction, to be " final," that it becomes the genetic fallacy.

Darwin's hypothesis, then, does not weaken the validity of religious ideas; the question of their truth or falsity remains in precisely the same position as always. It was only at first glance that Darwin appeared to be the enemy of God and the spirit. But there was a tendency in the nineteenth century to stop at the first glance, and so it turned out, as a matter of fact, that the force of Christian and theistic beliefs in general was greatly weakened in the Darwinian atmosphere. Correspondingly, the " scientific " tradition of thought was strengthened, and the conviction, typical of scientism, that science could explain everything, became increasingly current.

# 9

## Pragmatism and the Bourgeois Society

•

THE WORLD VIEW WHICH OB-
tained in the late nineteenth century was a product of the picture of the universe provided by Newton and the picture of
man delineated by Darwin. The world was a great machine,
material in nature and mechanical in behavior. Man was entirely the child of natural forces, his origin, development, and
character being solely due to the working of natural laws.

This view of things was furnished by the scientific method,
and was accepted more or less without question through the
power of the prevailing " scientific " climate of opinion. It was
undoubtedly true within limits, but was it the whole truth?
Two questions, at least, cried out for answers. First, is the naturalistic account of man the complete story? Can the empirical
method explain, for instance, the nature of human values which
men have always thought to have a reality of their own and to
exercise an influence over human behavior? How can values be
fitted into the nineteenth century world view? In the second
place, in what sense can this " scientific " metaphysics be said
to give the objective truth? Does it correspond with reality,
and if so, how on an empirical basis could we know this? Hume
had analyzed the concepts of substance and causality, which
were fundamental in this picture, in such a way as to show
that they were merely fictions, the " truth " of which could
never be discovered by means of the empirical method.

Two types of very similar philosophy attempted, in the nineteenth century, to meet these difficulties. Utilitarianism at-

140

tempted to solve the problem of values by showing that they also could be interpreted scientifically: terms like "right" and "good" can be defined empirically and thus brought within the purview of science. Pragmatism attempted to meet the problem of truth by showing that this concept also could be interpreted scientifically: terms like "true" and "false" can be defined empirically.

## Utilitarianism and Pragmatism

Utilitarianism was an English school of philosophy, whose leading exponent was J. S. Mill (1806–1873). Its main contribution to human thought was an ethical theory that attempted to explain ethical norms in empirical terms, to reduce the concepts of "good," "right," and "ought," which can have no scientific or empirical meaning, to the concepts of pleasure and utility, which have such a meaning.

Behind this ethical theory lay the assumption, typical of the age, that ethics, if it was to be an object of genuine knowledge, must be capable, like everything else, of scientific investigation. The procedure here, as in any other sphere of study, must consist of an examination of the facts, the formation of general laws on the basis of the facts, and the testing of these laws by further observation. In the case of ethics, the facts will be human behavior, and the general laws that are elicited will be the moral standards that we are seeking. In other words, Mill thought that by examining the way in which people actually behave, he would discover the way in which they ought to behave; or, rather, since "ought" is a term that has no scientific meaning, it must be ruled out of consideration.

On the basis of his observations of human behavior Mill claimed to have discovered the general ethical principle that governs and (which is for him the same thing) ought to govern our conduct.[1] This principle he called "utility or the greatest happiness principle." Utilitarianism, he said, is

"the creed which accepts as the foundation of morals utility or the greatest happiness principle, holds that actions are right in proportion as they tend to promote happiness, wrong as they tend to pro-

duce the reverse of happiness. By happiness is intended pleasure
and the absence of pain: by unhappiness is intended pain and the
privation of pleasure." [2]

This is a very ancient theory of ethics which is sometimes
also called Hedonism, and which goes back at least as far as
Athens in the fifth century B.C. It is also implicit in both Darwin
and Freud. What is good — that at which all men ought to aim
— is that at which all men, in fact, do aim, namely, pleasure;
and what is right is whatever is conducive to, or useful in obtaining, pleasure.

Thus, in utilitarianism, the ethical terms " good," " right,"
and " ought " have been reduced in meaning. The term " good "
is identical in meaning with the term " pleasure," and the term
" right " with the term " useful." Further, it is an empirical fact
that everyone acts in the way that he thinks will result in the
most pleasure, and since this is the general law of human behavior, it is the principle in accordance with which men
" ought " to act; and the phrase " ought to act " has been reduced in meaning to " do in fact act." Acting in order to
achieve the greatest amount of pleasure is the law of human
nature, like the laws of motion in physical nature, and " ought "
to be explained in exactly the same way.

The second problem for the nineteenth century " scientific "
world view had to do with the question, raised by Hume's analysis, of the objective truth of its fundamental concepts. The
concepts of substance and causality were fundamental because
the idea of substance was the essence of the materialistic assumption and the idea of cause and effect the basis of the
mechanistic axiom. But Hume pointed out that as long as we
remain strictly empirical, the most we can say for these notions
is that they are " useful fictions."

That these concepts were useful was proved by the enormous
successes that were achieved by science operating on the basis
of the quantitative and mechanical principles. Possibly inspired by the fact that Hume regarded " substance " and
" cause " as useful fictions and by the practical successes of the
scientific method, there arose, toward the end of the nineteenth

century, a new school of empirical philosophy called pragmatism which had its birthplace in the United States. Pragmatism, as it was developed by the American philosophers, William James (1842–1910) and John Dewey (1859–     ), attempted to perform the same service for the concept of " truth " as utilitarianism had performed for the concepts of " good " and " right." According to this theory, when Hume suggested that the fundamental scientific concepts were not " true " but merely " useful," he was contradicting himself. For to say that an idea or belief is true is simply to say that it is useful. In other words the term " true," like the term " right," can be reduced to " useful." The truth of a belief, like the rightness of an act, consists in nothing but its utility.

Pragmatism thus broke with the older type of empiricism, as found in Locke and Hume, which held that the function of an idea is to represent external reality, and that it was true when it corresponded to reality. William James denied this and maintained, rather, that the function of an idea is to lead to an experience of a certain kind, and that it is true when it successfully performs that function. In short, an idea is true if it works. When I entertain the idea of a table, for example, I do not have necessarily a representative mental image of the table. My idea may consist simply of words or signs which do not represent anything. At any rate the purpose of the idea, whatever its form, is to lead me to that type of sense experience which we call " table." The truth of an idea lies not in its ability to represent external reality but in its ability to lead to an experience of a certain kind. Truth, then, is nothing but utility or practical efficacy of this kind.

Pragmatism was here, obviously, making a further extension of Mill's utilitarian principle. Mill applied the principle to ethical values like " right " and concluded that an act is right when it is useful: James and Dewey applied it to the intellectual value called " truth " and concluded that a belief is true when it is useful. Thus any act may be called right and any belief true, if it *works*. " The true," said James, " to put it very briefly, is only the expedient in the way of our thinking, just as the right is only the expedient in the way of our behaving." [3]

The only difference between utilitarianism and pragmatism was in their answers to the question, " Expedient *for what?* " Utilitarianism answered, " Useful for obtaining pleasure." Pragmatism, however, understood that the identification of pleasure as *the* end of life, in reference to which all judgments were to be made, was a vast oversimplification; it contented itself with a vaguer answer: an act is right, or a belief true, if it is useful for achieving the purpose that an individual or group or society may happen to be entertaining.

The great accomplishment of pragmatism was its circumvention of Hume's criticism of empiricism's claim to truth. It achieved an impressive tour de force. For the truth of the basic concepts of empirical scientism was re-established by changing, not the definition of the concepts, but the definition of truth. Truth was no longer to be defined as correspondence with the facts, but as efficiency, expediency, utility.

Utilitarianism and pragmatism in regard to ethics and truth clearly constituted a philosophical reflection of one aspect of the " scientific " tradition, namely, its practical bent. At the very beginning of the modern period, Francis Bacon insisted that the aim of scientific knowledge was strictly utilitarian, that its function was to give man complete control over nature, and that this kind of knowledge was the only kind that was of any importance to man. It was only a short step (though it took three hundred years to complete) from saying that the most important kind of truth is that which is useful to saying that truth always and everywhere is nothing but " the expedient in the way of our thinking." Science is only interested in beliefs that are true in the sense that they work. Pragmatism simply took the next step which consisted of saying that this is the definition of truth as such. Similarly, science is only interested in actions that are right in the sense that they work. Utilitarianism simply took the next step, which consisted of saying that this is the definition of right as such. Pragmatism and utilitarianism both belong to the same line of development and are clearly philosophical expressions of the " scientific " age.

The relativistic implications for both conduct and belief are obvious. There are no universally valid criteria in reference to which a distinction can be made between right and wrong or between true and false. Any act is right and any belief is true that happens to serve the purpose of the individual or the group. Success in this function is all that matters. Instead of universal standards which remain over and above all human purposes, the only standard of what is right and of what is true is the furtherance of human aims. Man now makes the pretension to be the master and not the servant of the true and the good. Empirical scientism is developing in the direction of its more arrogant brothers.

A further development of the same kind is apparent in the twentieth century successor of utilitarianism and pragmatism, which is popularly known as logical positivism. This contemporary school is largely preoccupied with the new science of semantics or semeiotics, which investigates the nature of signs and their interrelationship in language. In other words, it goes behind the investigation of the meaning of " right " and " true " and examines the meaning of " meaning." It asserts that the sole criterion of meaning is verifiability in sense experience. It insists dogmatically, as a final and unassailable dictum, that a statement has meaning if, and only if, there is some empirical method of testing that is relevant to the establishment of its truth or falsity. All other alleged statements (except the propositions of logic and mathematics [4]) have no meaning at at all and are therefore literally nonsense. If someone asserts, for instance, that beauty is truth, then, since no empirical investigation would contribute in the least to proving it true or false, this particular collection of words is an unintelligible " pseudo statement."

If, in connection with Hume's criticism, pragmatism accomplished a mighty tour de force by redefining the concept of truth, the ingenuity of its achievement pales into insignificance in comparison with the efforts of logical positivism. This philosophy, by its definition of meaning, restricts the area of the meaningful to the empirically verifiable, and thereby, of course, renders outstanding service to the cause of scientism. On this view, we cannot talk meaningfully about anything except the physical realm which is, undoubtedly, the sphere of science. Not only is it the case, as we have heard often before, that science alone can give us real truth and genuine knowledge, but it now appears that only science is capable of making statements that have any meaning.

Metaphysics, ethics, poetry, art, and religion — man's "higher nature" — which Marx castigated as mere ideological rationalization of the existing economy and Freud as nothing but projections of repressed sexuality, are now dismissed as simply grandiloquent nonsense. On the positive side, they are accounted for as expressions of emotion. When such emotional ejaculations are seriously advanced as descriptions of reality, they are to be rejected out of hand as " spurious " and " bogus."

All this is clearly in the tradition of scientism. If Hume took empirical scientism to one of its logical conclusions in extreme skepticism, logical positivism develops it to its only other possible end result in dogmatism. Science is established in a position of unrivaled supremacy as the reigning sovereign of the human understanding.

### Agnosticism

Empirical scientism first of all reduces all value words to empirically testable terms like " pleasure " and " utility," and finally rejects them altogether as merely subjective and emotional. Its treatment of religious belief follows the same course; in the end the traditional religious world view is dismissed as literally nonsense and is replaced by the scientific *Weltanschauung,* or the religion of science.

In the nineteenth century J. S. Mill and T. H. Huxley ( 1825–1895 ) carried farther forward the demand of Locke and the Deists, in the previous century, that the beliefs of religion must be susceptible of the same kind of empirical validation as scientific hypotheses, and if unsuccessful in meeting this test must be rejected. Mill applied the empirical method to belief in the existence and nature of God. He began by examining all the evidence for and against belief in God, and concluded that there was insufficient to settle the question conclusively.[5] The only scientifically proper course, therefore, is to suspend judgment. In regard to the Christian belief that God is both all-good and all-powerful, he decided that the evidence is conclusively against the proposition. The amount of evil that exists in the world proves that God cannot be both all-good and all-powerful, for if he were, he both *would* and *could* abolish evil. The fact that he fails to do so shows either that he is all-good and *wants* to abolish evil but *cannot,* and therefore is not all-powerful, or else that he is all-powerful and *could* abolish evil but does not *want* to, and therefore is not all-good.[6]

Mill asserted that all religious beliefs fall into one of two classes. Either the evidence is insufficient to settle the matter and they cannot be accepted as true or the evidence is conclusively against them and they must be rejected as false. In any case, according to Mill, it is quite unnecessary to answer the questions that religion raises, for the empirical method of science is quite adequate to solve all problems and to provide a satisfactory life for man without any appeal to a deity, of whose nature and even existence we can never be certain.[7] Mill did not deny dogmatically either the propriety of the questions that religion asks nor the possible validity of some of its answers. He never categorically asserted that the belief in God is either meaningless or false, and sometimes, like Feuerbach, seems to have been on the verge of recommending its adoption as morally *useful.*[8] He contented himself with noting, first, that in general the evidence is insufficient to settle these questions, and, secondly, that in any case it is for the most part unnecessary to adopt such beliefs since science itself can secure the good life for man on earth.

T. H. Huxley treated religion in much the same way, but expressed himself in rather more violent language. In his view, it is both scientifically improper and morally dishonest to hold beliefs the nature of which is such that the human mind is never likely to discover any decisive empirical evidence in their favor.

" The foundation of morality is to have done, once and for all, with lying; to give up pretending to believe that for which there is no evidence, and repeating unintelligible propositions about things beyond the possibilities of knowledge." [9]

The only ethically honest attitude toward the questions that religion tries to answer is, " I don't know." And from the Greek word for " not knowing " Huxley coined the word " agnostic " to describe this position.

Agnostics are obviously not theists, for they do not assert that God exists; but neither are they atheists, for they do not deny that God exists. In principle they are restricted to saying, " We do not know." In practice, however, they find it difficult to refrain from going farther. They strongly suspect that no one else knows; often, as in the case of Huxley, they are annoyed at anyone who says he does know and who insists on adopting religious beliefs. They are filled with righteous indignation and their moral sense is outraged when confronted with such an unscientific attitude. They brand it as " immoral," since " immoral " is for them synonymous with " unscientific," and " moral " with " scientific." Science is coming to be regarded as the author not only of all truth, knowledge, and power, but also of all ethical values as well. For these nineteenth century agnostics limited their skepticism to religion: in regard to science they exhibited the most wholehearted and unswerving faith, which, while impressive in its unquestioning devotion, was nevertheless, in the light of subsequent history, somewhat naïve.

Pragmatism in general continued to develop this attitude of rather hostile agnosticism toward religion, accompanied by blind faith in science. An exception, however, was William James, who considered that certain religious beliefs are in the nature of what he called " forced options " and that certain " extraempirical " beliefs are essential to full understanding and to the good life. This momentary lapse from the true scientific faith was soon corrected by James's followers in the pragmatic camp. Thus Dewey asserted that religious beliefs are " at war with the habits of mind congruous . . . with science " and must therefore, of course, be abolished.[10] "The modern spirit . . . puts away the supernaturalism of the race's immaturity and relies upon the resources of the scientific search for truth."[11]

In logical positivism this hostility reaches its culmination, as far as this type of scientism is concerned, with the dismissal of all religious statements as nonsensical. Such statements do not attain the status of being improbable (Mill) or morally dishonest (Huxley) or even false (Dewey); they are entirely meaningless. Thus this school goes behind the positions of both agnosticism and atheism and maintains that it is impossible to say anything significant whatever about God. "All utterances about the nature of God are nonsensical."[12]

Utilitarianism, pragmatism, and logical positivism, all typical products of Anglo-Saxon culture in the nineteenth and twentieth centuries, agree in ruling out nonempirical and nonphysical beliefs of every kind as either extremely doubtful, downright false, or literally meaningless. Empirical scientism rejects the traditional world view or religion of the West. This is its negative contribution. On the positive side, however, it has a religion of its own. This new religion is the religion of science. It puts science in the place of God. The former, rather than the latter, is now regarded as omniscient — the giver of all truth; as omnipotent — the source of all power; as absolutely good — the arbiter of all moral standards; and finally as the savior — the guarantor of salvation for all mankind. The worshipers of this god unquestioningly accept its revelations as the absolute truth about reality. Thus Mill and Huxley enthusiastically and without question adopted the picture of the universe given by nineteenth century physics as the final truth about reality. Reality was a great physical machine which was entirely governed by fixed natural laws and which embraced everything, including human thought and behavior, in its majestic if somewhat metallic and altogether mechanical embrace.

Concerning this nineteenth century world view, Paul Elmer More has written:

" There was indeed at first sight a seductive simplicity about the theories of Huxley and his militant brothers. It is so easy to say that the world is nothing but a machine nicely constructed of atoms, running smoothly and undeviatingly under the mechanical laws of motion; to deny that anything new or incalculable ever breaks in to disarrange the regularity demanded by science; to dispose of the appetites and passions and very consciousness of man as mere products of atomical reaction. It was the kind of simplification that promised to solve for us all the annoying problems of life. . . . Certainly if any group of men had a cosmic foot rule in their pockets, it was this particular group of mid-Victorians." [13]

The religious veneration of science as all-good, all-knowing, and all-powerful, which was characteristic of Huxley and others in the nineteenth century, is maintained by pragmatists and logical positivists in the twentieth. Thus Dewey explicitly equated the scientific spirit with genuine " religion ": " Science," he said, " has the same spiritual import as supernaturalism," [14] and again, " The religious values are implicit in the spirit of science." [15] Speaking for logical positivism, A. J. Ayer says, " There is no field of experience which cannot, in principle, be brought under some form of scientific law and no type of speculative knowledge which it is, in principle, beyond the power of science to give." [16] In other words, science is omniscience, and when all its reports are at last brought together and systematically applied in every area of life, then its proper function as man's omnipotent savior will be realized.[17]

## Capitalism

Anglo-Saxon thought, as we have traced it, is clearly in the same " scientific " tradition that has produced Marxism and the Communist state, and the Nazi ideology with its barbarism. In our culture, this tradition is responsible for the empiricistic biases of our philosophy, the utilitarian character of our ethics, our pragmatic conception of truth, our agnosticism in regard to God, and our religious devotion to science. It remains to trace the general features of the capitalistic, bourgeois society which this way of thinking produced in the Western democracies.

Nineteenth century Anglo-Saxon society was a politico-economic reflection of the same assumptions of which utilitarianism and pragmatism were the philosophical articulation, and devotion to science the religious expression. This kind of philosophy and " religion " was an obvious product of empirical scientism. But how did industrial capitalism fit into this same general picture?

Nothing is easier than to show the connection between utilitarianism and industrial capitalism in Great Britain. For Mill and his followers aligned themselves quite explicitly with Adam Smith, Ricardo, and the Manchester school as the spokesman for laissez-faire liberalism and capitalism. It is rather surprising for us to discover that in doing so they were regarded in their day as " radicals." The reason for this is that in the first part of the nineteenth century the landed aristocracy still preserved their special privileges and power in England. The new industrialist class, later to be known as capitalist, was just beginning to make its weight felt, and its drive for power was something new and radical at that time. The political " radicals " were those who championed this new industrialist class against the old semifeudal aristocracy.

Once the industrial revolution began to take its effect in the nineteenth century it was, of course, in the interest of the new industrial class in society to have a laissez-faire economy, an economy in which the Government did not interfere but rather allowed economic forces free play. The economists of the Manchester school were attempting to justify an unplanned free economy in terms of certain alleged economic laws like that of supply and demand. They believed that these economic laws, by their automatic and mechanical operation, would establish a just and satisfactory economy, in much the same way that the laws of motion govern the universe without any assistance from man.

It was quite obvious to Mill, as indeed it is to anyone, that laissez-faire liberalism not only fits in with the Newtonian physics but is also the political and economic application of the utilitarian pleasure-principle in ethics, with its individualistic and " do-as-you-please " implications. For Mill, society was just a collection of individuals, as nature is just a collection of atoms; indeed the word *individuum* is the Latin translation of the Greek word *atomos*. And just as the behavior of atoms in nature is governed mechanically by certain natural laws, so the economy of human society should be allowed to function " naturally " in accordance with economic laws. Government exists only to protect the individual and his right to life, liberty, and the pursuit of happiness (that is, pleasure). It should deal with its citizens as so many individual units, each equally capable of pleasure. The sole duty of the government is to see that there are no barriers in the way of each one's achieving his fair share of pleasure. Above all, it must refrain from placing any restrictions on the political and economic liberty of individuals, except those that are necessary to insure that no individual or minority is obtaining pleasure at the expense of inflicting pain or deprivation on others. The only such group that appeared to constitute a threat of this kind in the early part of the nineteenth century was the landed aristocracy. According to Mill, therefore, it was the duty of the Government to limit the activities, privileges, and power of this group, but to refrain from all other interference, and everywhere else to permit the free play of the pleasure-principle and the laws of economy.

A hundred years ago Mill and his followers were already employing all the familiar arguments in favor of free enterprise and against Government interference, planning, and controls. All Government interference is an infringement of individual liberty. Any action which is performed as a result of Government compulsion rather than by free choice not only violates liberty but decreases skill and efficiency. Bentham, who was Mill's intellectual father, even went so far as to object to the erection of lighthouses by the Government, on the ground that they interfered with the navigator's free enterprise in choosing his course and consequently contributed to inferior skill in navigation. This illustration, while of course an extreme case, nevertheless serves to underscore the utilitarians' insistence that the powers of the Government be kept to a bare minimum. All that the Government was required to do was to see that the individual was enabled to act as he economically pleased, in so far as he did not prevent others from doing as they pleased. The individual must be allowed complete freedom of economic action, and this, of course, was interpreted to mean that the individual must be left free to make as much money as he could. Following the Manchester school, Mill was confident that completely free enterprise and unrestricted economic competition would operate automatically for the greatest happiness of the greatest number. This confidence was based on the belief that there are certain economic laws which, like the laws of nature, operate mechanically for the long-range benefit of all concerned.[18]

Mill's political and economic theory made him the intellectual champion of the new industrialist or capitalist class in nineteenth century Britain and the philosophical spokesman for laissez-faire liberalism in British politics. His political and economic ideas in turn stemmed from his devotion to Newtonian physics as the clue to the nature of reality in general and from his utilitarian position in regard to ethics. Utilitarianism and laissez-faire liberalism were both offspring of the " scientific " tradition.

Another way of showing the connection between the modern " scientific " frame of reference and the nineteenth century capitalistic economic structure is to point out, with Bertrand Russell, that industrialism, which fathered the capitalist class, is simply " science in the sphere of practice." [19] Science gave us the industrial revolution and scientism a utilitarian ethics. When the former developed within the context of the latter, the industrialist rose to a dominant position in society and the machines were introduced, not primarily to meet the needs of all classes, but simply with a view to making money for their owners.

Finally, there is an intimate relationship between pragmatism and industrial capitalism. Russell suggests that the former is precisely " the philosophy appropriate to industrialism," [20] and both of course are related to science:

" Science is becoming increasingly a manner of life, a way of behaving, and is developing a philosophy which substitutes for the old conception of knowledge the new conception of successful behavior. . . . This is likely to become true throughout the world, but for the moment it is of course more true in a country like America where the practical success of science is very evident." [21]

The U.S.A. is pre-eminently the land where the man who " gets results " is the most highly esteemed, and where the man who makes money is alone regarded as " successful." In this country, above all, efficiency, technical excellence, and mechanical ingenuity have combined to produce a complex, technological social structure. This highly industrialized and commercialized society is the social reflection of empirical scientism. The philosophical voice of both of these phenomena is pragmatism, which teaches that whatever works, gets things done, and solves practical problems is right and true.

There is no intention of deprecating here the extent to which science, industrialization, and laissez-faire capitalism have added to man's material welfare. There can be no question but that scientific progress has resulted in tremendous gains in man's knowledge and power in relation to nature. Dazzling victories have been won over space, time, disease, scarcity, and over a host of evils and limitations that were previously thought to constitute a permanent part of man's earthly lot.

Secondly, the industrial revolution, which was achieved by the application of science to economic problems, has more and more eased and increased the production of material goods. The substitution of the machine for manual labor has both released men from many types of backbreaking drudgery and also technically solved the problem of meeting the physical needs of the whole human race.

In the third place, the capitalistic economic structure, with its free enterprise and unrestricted competition, in spite of its subsequently revealed defects, was unquestionably, at the outset, the best way of developing the potentialities of industrialism and of spreading its benefits as widely as possible. It was capitalism that raised the standard of living in the West to unprecedented levels. At the same time, the principles of capitalistic theory gave economic expression to the political ideals of advancing democracy, with its emphasis on the freedom and rights of the individual.

All these gains were made possible by three great benefactions: science gave us knowledge; industrialism put it to work; capitalism spread its benefits. No wonder, then, that science, as the type of modern knowledge; the machine, as the symbol of modern technology; and the dollar, as the lodestar of capitalism, came to be worshiped almost as gods and to combine together as the trinity of a new secular religion.

The relationship between these gods has been shown by R. S. Lynd:

" Edison, Ford, the Wright brothers — men like these, aided of course by American business enterprise — were the great creators, and American boys have placed such men with the political giants . . . as the ' great Americans.' An increasing stream of able young scientists flowed into the private laboratories of General Electric, United States Steel, duPont and other corporations. . . . A world of enterprising businessmen which bought invention and efficiency by giving subsidies to science appeared to be the latest and happiest formula in that succession of lucky circumstances known as ' the American way.' " [22]

It was all three of these beneficent powers that were responsible for the great advances of the age;

"but to the average citizen it seemed enough to say that they happened because men had been left free to make money. . . . The formula is deceptively simple: welfare is a more or less automatic by-product of money-making: and if men will but apply themselves to the instrumental activity of earning more and more money, that is the best and surest way to achieve the quantitative ends of living we are all after." [23]

Industrialism and pragmatism combined to exalt the dollar to divine status. The former raised the owners of the machines to a predominant position in society and at the same time put more material goods into the hands of more people. The result was that the values of the industrialist, which appeared also to be responsible for raising the whole standard of living, became the prevailing values of the culture. But the industrialist, as such, operates on a purely utilitarian or pragmatic basis. He is interested in solving practical problems, and in securing the maximum of human and mechanical efficiency. What is right in behavior and true in theory is what is useful in practice. And if the question is raised, "Useful for what?" the answer is now ready at hand: "Useful for making money." This becomes the very concrete end which the whole society pursues, and in reference to which all judgments are passed.

The dominant factors in nineteenth century Anglo-Saxon society were thus industry, commerce, economics, and money. This veneration of the dollar as the highest value in life is the justification for applying the adjective "bourgeois" to this culture. According to *The Oxford English Dictionary*, this word means "pertaining to the mercantile class." To say that a society is bourgeois is to say that its whole culture is commercialized and that there the dollar reigns supreme. It is a society, as someone has said, that knows the price of everything and the value of nothing.

Materialistic scientism produced the Communist society, which is a type of economic collectivism. Naturalistic scientism produced the Nazi society, which is a kind of instinctual barbarism. Empirical scientism has given rise to a bourgeois society, which worships science, the machine, and the dollar. And just as empirical scientism must either deteriorate into complete skepticism or else harden into a dogmatic mold that resembles the other two versions, so also the culture that it nurtures is faced with only two alternatives: either it will disintegrate in aimlessness and confusion or else it will petrify into some kind of "scientific" mass society.

# 10

## Empirical Scientism

•

THE CRITICISM OF THE PHILOS-
ophy of empirical scientism begins, as in the case of the other
versions, by showing that its doctrines are not independently
arrived at but are simply the conclusions of more or less uncritically accepted presuppositions, which, in turn, are provided by the prevailing climate of opinion. The next step is an
attempt to show that these doctrines are, in any case, fallacious. And finally, the disastrous social fruits of this way of
thinking, while not sufficient by themselves to prove its falsity
(except on the merely pragmatic criterion of truth), nevertheless bring it under strong suspicion.

### Criticism of Its Doctrines

Mill's utilitarianism was an attempt to explain the value
words "good" and "right" empirically in terms of pleasure
and utility. This familiar procedure of reducing ethical terms
to "natural" meanings, accompanied by the claim that no loss
of significance is involved, is an application to this area of life
of the empiricistic bias, which is the tendency to assume that
the scientific method can explain everything. The result is an
illustration of the general rule that the findings of an investigator are determined by the method that he uses. If he encounters factors in his field that his method is incapable of
handling, he must either dismiss them as illusions or reduce
them to terms that his method can understand.

One of the difficulties in Mill's reduction of "good" to

157

"pleasure" is that, if the identification were complete, it is hard to understand how the well-known moral conflict between duty and inclination could ever arise. If what I ought to do is always what is most pleasant, how could it come about that sometimes I *want* to do one thing yet feel *obliged* to do another? Mill attempted to solve the problem by saying that the rule for human behavior is really to "act in such a way as to procure the *greatest amount* of pleasure in the long run and for the greatest number of people." This principle certainly seems to explain, in empirical and "natural" terms, that kind of apparently moral struggle which turns out, on closer examination, to be actually just a conflict between my desire for some immediate pleasure and my desire for some greater pleasure in the future: "I should like to knock off and have a cup of coffee, but I ought to go on working (in order to gain the satisfaction of completing my task)."

The same principle was meant to account for the other type of conflict which is more genuinely moral. I sometimes feel that I ought to sacrifice my own pleasure in the interests of others. Mill thought that he had explained such situations in terms of his own theory by pointing out that what is involved is still the greatest amount of pleasure. In gaining pleasure for myself, I may prevent a great many other people from gaining pleasure, and so detract from the highest possible total of pleasure. Such an act would be wrong, and I ought not to do it.

This account, however, obviously fails to explain away the troublesome concept of obligation. The theory that what men ought to do is really what they want to do, and that what they want to do is to achieve the greatest amount of pleasure, derives its plausibility from the fact that men do, for the most part, desire their *own* greatest pleasure. They do not, however, "naturally" desire the greatest pleasure of *others*. When they sacrifice their own pleasure in the interests of others, they do so from a sense of obligation, which cannot be reduced, without loss of meaning, to "desire for pleasure." It might be replied that the greatest pleasure of the greatest number, that is, the welfare of society in general, does contribute to my own greatest pleasure in the long run. But is this really a convincing explanation of the fact that occasionally a man lays down his life for his friend? It is the sense of duty to our fellows and to society that causes us, at least now and then, to act against our own interests.

Freudianism, which is also based on the pleasure-principle, attempted (without success, as we tried to show) a more elaborate "scientific" analysis of social obligation in terms of repression and projection. But as far as utilitarianism is concerned, this ethical concept certainly survives the alleged reduction.

As for the reduction of "the good" to pleasure and "the right" to utility, it is enough to point out that we can always ask concerning any pleasure whether it is good and concerning anything expedient whether it is right. These questions would, of course, be impossible if the terms were synonymous. As in the case of obligation, so in the case of the right and the good, the reductions are not accomplished without loss of meaning.

Pragmatism tried to handle the value term "truth" in the same way and with the same results. No doubt the pragmatic definition of truth in terms of utility is satisfactory for the practical purposes of science. And since in a "scientific" age scientific activity is regarded as the normative discipline, it is taken for granted that this scientific or pragmatic test of truth is the only criterion. But is this really the case? When we ask for the truth about reality, we are asking what reality is really like and not which beliefs about it would be useful in practice. Practical scientists may be interested only in the latter question, and usefulness is therefore all that they require of their beliefs. Nevertheless, it is permissible, and indeed it is one of the distinguishing characteristics of man, to be interested also in the former question, in which case something more than utility is needed for an adequate definition of truth.

This reduction of values leads of course to relativism. If acts are right and beliefs are true only when they are useful, the question is, "Useful for what?" The answer of pragmatism is, "Useful for achieving the agent's purpose." The anarchical implications of such ethical individualism are avoided by introducing the purposes of society as a whole. But then the anarchy is simply transferred to the international level. Each particular society becomes its own arbiter of what is right and true. Those acts are right and those beliefs are true that are conducive to its given purposes. The behavior of contemporary totalitarianism is thus entirely justified by a theory that was produced in the Anglo-Saxon democracies. According to this theory, if the U.S.S.R. and the U.S.A. define the word " democracy " in different ways, there can be no dispute as to which definition is " really " true; both definitions are true in the sense that they serve the different purposes of the two societies. As a matter of fact, of course, neither of these societies is prepared to admit this conclusion, although both are more or less committed to pragmatism. Each is actually convinced that there is a question of objective truth at stake and that this truth is *not* a matter of mere utility.

Apart from these unwelcome practical implications, any thoroughgoing relativism is self-refuting. If relativism claims to be absolutely true, it is implicitly claiming that this is one truth that is not relative. On the other hand, if it purports to be only relatively true, we should be glad to agree. For there can be no doubt that *our convictions* as to what is good and right and true are relative to a host of sociological and psychological factors. This means, however, not that there are no objective and universal values, but only that our comprehension of them is always distorted, partial, and incomplete.

As far as logical positivism is concerned, everything depends on its definition of meaning. It is this definition that rules out metaphysics, theology, ethics, and art. But the identification of meaning with verifiability in sense experience is obviously the result of the presuppositions of the " scientific " frame of reference. In the case of this philosophy, more clearly than in any other, these presuppositions determine the nature of the conclusions. One of these assumptions is that the physical is alone knowable. When the concept of meaning is examined with this bias in mind, it must inevitably be defined as empirical verifiability.

This is certainly the criterion of meaning *for science*. But it is only on the basis of the empiricistic assumption, to the effect that science alone gives truth, that this criterion could have been regarded as definitive for *all* human communication. Surely no one, except a victim of scientism, could seriously suggest, nor any age except a " scientific " age for a moment accept the suggestion, that Plato's *Republic* and Tolstoy's *War and Peace* are mixtures of syntactical confusions and prolonged emotional ejaculations. The fact is that the empirically verifiable propositions of science are the most exact and precise that the human mind can formulate. But science achieves these results by abstracting and isolating the more superficial aspects of reality and ignoring its heights and depths.

## Criticism of Its Agnosticism

Nineteenth century empirical scientism worshiped science, the machine, and the dollar. But as long as it remained *empirical* and kept its eyes open to the facts, it was bound sooner or later to be disillusioned as to the divine nature of these powers. It was bound to realize eventually that the " scientific " world view is profoundly depressing, and leads in the end to pessimism, despair, and radical skepticism. On the other hand, if it insists on retaining the basic doctrines of *scientism*, it will become more and more dogmatic, until it issues into something that resembles the materialistic, economic version.

The earlier devotees of the religion of science were confident that the universe was a great machine, operating in accordance with inexorable laws. Secure in this predictable environment, and believing that human progress was guaranteed by science and evolution, they were confident and optimistic. By the end of the century, however, other less superficial and more sensitive observers, while still unable to transcend this " scientific " metaphysics, began to understand that if it were the whole and final truth, then the proper attitude of man is pessimism and despair.

Bertrand Russell, in a well-known essay written in 1903, emphasized the fact that " the world which science presents for

our belief is even more purposeless, more void of meaning "
than that which Mephistopheles described to Dr. Faustus:

" That man is the product of causes which had no prevision of the
end they were achieving; that his origin, his growth, his hopes and
fears, his loves and beliefs, are but the outcome of accidental collo-
cations of atoms; that no fire, no heroism, no intensity of thought
and feeling can preserve an individual life beyond the grave; that
all the labors of the ages, all the devotion, all the inspiration, all the
noonday brightness of human genius, are destined to extinction in
the vast death of the solar system, and that the whole temple of
man's achievement must inevitably be buried beneath the debris of
a universe in ruins — all these, if not quite beyond dispute, are yet so
nearly certain that no philosophy which rejects them can hope to
stand."

Little wonder, then, that Russell concluded:

" Only on the firm foundation of unyielding despair can the soul's
habitation be safely built. . . . The life of man is a long march
through the night, surrounded by invisible foes, tortured by weari-
ness and pain, towards a goal that few can hope to reach, and where
none may tarry long. . . . Brief and powerless is man's life; on him
and all his race the slow sure doom falls pitiless and dark. Blind to
good and evil, reckless of destruction, omnipotent matter rolls on its
relentless way; for man, condemned today to lose his dearest, to-
morrow himself to pass through the gate of darkness, it remains only
to cherish, ere yet the blow falls, the lofty thoughts which ennoble
his little day . . . proudly defiant of the irresistible forces that tol-
erate, for a moment, his knowledge and his condemnation, to sus-
tain alone, a weary but unyielding Atlas, the world that his own
ideals have fashioned despite the trampling march of unconscious
power." [1]

Another passage, from an essay written in the same period by
R. L. Stevenson, reveals the horror and disgust that many were
beginning to feel in the face of the sordid implications of the
" scientific " view of the universe and of life:

" We behold space sown with rotatory islands, seas and worlds and
shards and wrecks of systems; some, like the sun, still blazing; some
rotting, like the earth; others, like the moon, stable in desolation.
All of these we take to be made of something we call matter. . . .
This stuff, when not purified by the lustration of fire, rots uncleanly
into something we call life; seized through all its atoms with a pedic-

ulous malady; swelling in tumors which become independent, sometimes even (by a horrid prodigy) locomotory. . . . And to put the
last touch on this mountain mass of the revolting and the inconceiv-
able, all these prey upon each other, lives tearing other lives in
pieces, cramming them inside themselves, and, by that summary
process, growing fat. . . . What a monstrous spectre is this man,
the disease of the agglutinated dust." [2]

The pessimism and despair induced by a realistic appreciation of the implications of the "scientific" *Weltanschauung*
were reinforced by the course of human history and of scientific progress in the twentieth century. For the story of this
century, since 1914, has been a chronicle of disasters: the First
World War, the economic collapse, the breakdown of the
League of Nations, the Second World War, the "cold war"
between the Communist states and the nations of the Atlantic
Pact, and, hovering over all, the awful threat of the atomic
bomb.

The atomic bomb is only the latest and most vivid example
of the double potentialities of scientific progress. All the discoveries and inventions of science have enormous possibilities
both for good and for evil. The printing press and the radio
can be used for educational purposes, but also in the service
of yellow journalism and propaganda. The motor car not only
facilitates transportation, but also takes the form of a highly
effective lethal weapon. The airplane reduces the barriers of
space and time, but is also useful for dropping bombs. The
control of bacteria is an instrument for spreading both health
and disease. This list could be enlarged indefinitely. The point
is that science, which makes possible these various alternatives,
in no way discriminates between them; it offers no standard of
values. The ancient human problem of the choice between good
and evil, far from being solved by science, is simply intensified
by every advance in scientific knowledge and power. Science
cannot provide the wisdom that would enable man to control
the power that it places in his hands.

"Where shall wisdom be found? and where is the place of
understanding?" [3] If science fails us at this crucial point, where

shall we look for salvation? The answer is, "Nowhere," for science was our god, and we know now that its feet are made of clay.

This despair is finally augmented by a radical skepticism about the truth of science itself. The quantum and relativity theories have upset the fundamental assumptions of nineteenth century physics and have thereby destroyed the foundation of the religion of science. It now appears that Newton's materialistic-mechanistic universe was hopelessly oversimplified. Matter itself, as solid, extended, substantial stuff, tends increasingly to dissolve away, and we are left with we know not what as the primary constituents of the universe. Nor can we, any longer, pay unswerving devotion to the concept of mechanical law as the clue to the secrets of nature. We are now told that there is something unpredictable about the behavior of the atoms, which means that the formulas of physics are no longer regarded as mechanical laws but simply as statistical averages. In other words, both the quantitative and the mechanical principles of science itself are being examined afresh. "The stable foundations of physics," writes A. N. Whitehead, "have broken up . . . the old foundations of scientific thought are becoming unintelligible." [4]

The basic materialistic and mechanistic assumptions of the prevailing "scientific" tradition of thought and of the religion of science are thus called in question. The "scientific" age loses its last remaining faith. The weapons that empirical scientism had turned against the traditional religion of the West are now turned against the religion of science. The plain man, who had absorbed that earlier agnosticism in regard to God, is now the victim of this new and more thoroughgoing skepticism which David Hume long ago foresaw.

If materialistic scientism leads to Marxism and the "economic man," and naturalistic scientism to Nazism and the "faceless man," then one of the logical conclusions of empirical scientism in the Anglo-Saxon world is certainly radical skepticism and the "hollow man" [5] — the man who believes in nothing, not even in himself.

## Science as the Key of Knowledge

While skepticism and the "hollow man" seem to be the most typical twentieth century products of empirical scientism, it is also possible that a further development of scientism proper still lies in wait for the Western world. Skepticism is a vacuum that sooner or later must be filled. If the more positive and dynamic creed that is to replace it takes the form of intensified scientism, in spite of all the factors just rehearsed that ought to militate against it, it is altogether probable that it will develop into something, by some other name, that resembles Marxism. For Marxism, after all, is the clearest and most consistent articulation of the biases of the "scientific" tradition. Furthermore, there are certain tendencies in our way of thinking and in our bourgeois society that need only to be carried farther forward in the same direction to result in Marxist dogmas and economic collectivism. Indeed, it might be said that Marxist Communism, or something very like it, is precisely what a "scientific" age deserves.

First of all, on the level of ideas, the materialistic and atheistic scientism of Marx is closely related to the empirical and agnostic scientism of the Anglo-Saxon world. Marx himself was not really a rebel against Western "scientific" civilization; he was its child. As a matter of fact, he openly acknowledged his debt to Anglo-Saxon philosophy. "Materialism," he said, "is the natural-born son of Great Britain." [6] And he went on to mention Bacon, Locke, and Hobbes, in particular, as his philosophical forebears. Empiricism implicitly assumes that the physical is alone knowable; it is but a short step to the dogma that matter is the primary reality.

In the same passage, Marx referred to the English Deists and pointed out, quite rightly, that Deism is just "an easygoing way of getting rid of religion." And if Deism undermined the traditional faith of the West, the agnosticism of the following century was another step in the direction of its abolition. Agnosticism, in any case, as Engels said,[7] is simply "polite atheism"; it is the Anglo-Saxon brand of atheism, which, for all practical purposes, simply disregards the existence of God. And in Great Britain, as Engels went on to say, agnosticism is just as respectable as the Church of England, and definitely a step above the Salvation Army.

Similarly, the Darwinian theory of man and the pragmatic theory of values are very much in harmony with the materialistic interpretation of human life. Pragmatic relativism needs only to be given a slight twist to turn into the Marxist economic version. In the same way, the belief in determinism, which has grown up in the West as the prestige of sociology and psychology has increased without any accompanying awareness of their limitations, needs only to be developed in one direction to become the dogma of absolute economic determinism.

This kind of development of Western relativism and determinism is rendered all the more probable when it is understood that Marx's economic determinism was little more than a translation into metaphysical terms of the Anglo-Saxon worship of the dollar and exaltation of economic power. Economism, which thinks of economic forces as all-powerful, is common both to bourgeois practice and to Communist theory. Worship of the dollar as the highest value in life leads on to the worship of economic forces as all-powerful; it was a bourgeois society that first of all destroyed all values except the commercial. Further, it was a capitalistic society, as Berdyaev has said, in which "the imperious and inhuman power of money . . . determined the fate of man."[8] Under the seemingly relentless sway of economic law, the individual was helpless and the condition of his society was impersonally determined. "It is not Marx who is to blame for this perversion. Marx discovered this idea in the capitalistic bourgeois society of the nineteenth century."[9]

Another factor in our own society that points in the direction of the collectivist state is the process of standardization which is fostered by expanding industrialism. The mechanization of the means of production and distribution bore magnificent fruits, but, like Frankenstein's invention, the machine as it grows in power, threatens the life of its inventor with its heavy mechanical hand. The fruit of the industrial revolution in the West is the hideous factory city, within which men cease to be human persons and become mere standardized units. During their working hours they serve the machines in meaningless and monotonous toil, and the rest of the time are beaten into sterile uniformity both by the mass-produced goods of the machines and by the commercialized exploitation of the new techniques of mass communication. They are herded together in close quarters, where they live in identical houses, surrounded by identical furnishings, and dressed in identical clothes. At the same time, under the influence of newspaper chains, popular magazines, best sellers, book clubs, moving pictures, radio and television programs, they all come to think along the same stereotyped lines. The degree of standardization that is thus unconsciously imposed by a highly industrialized society, like the U.S.A., is scarcely less than that which is deliberately induced by a totalitarian state, like the U.S.S.R.

The mass society that scientism and industrial capitalism have produced in the West bears striking similarities to the mass society that Marxism and totalitarian Communism have fashioned in Russia. According to Kathleen Bliss,

" this resemblance is rooted in certain fundamental characteristics of the modern world which neither has escaped. They both suffer from giganticism. They both show unquestioning confidence in the scientist and the technocrat. They both accept a materialistic conception of civilization. They both tend — one consciously, the other unconsciously — to exclude from life the personal, the spiritual . . . without which man's hold even on his essential humanity seems to grow feeble." [10]

It seems that Marx was right when he said that nineteenth century capitalistic society had within it the seeds of its own destruction. What he did not understand was that these same seeds grow to maturity in the Communist totalitarian state of which he himself was the sponsor. Communism is not an inexplicable aberration in the history of modern civilization; it is not a radical departure from the main line of development;

it is, rather, the logical culmination and natural climax of a host of tendencies and assumptions that began as far back as the sixteenth century. Western culture, with its secularism, standardization, and commercialism, and Communist society, with its atheism, regimentation, and economism, are blood brothers and children of that same "scientific" tradition of thought and life that has been the prevailing influence in the whole modern period of history.

Marxist Communism is simply a more extreme version of Western secularism, and points the way which it too may eventually follow. The more moderate beliefs of empirical scientism may harden into all-embracing dogmas: empiricism into materialism, agnosticism into atheism, vague relativism and determinism into forthright economic determinism, and the general belief in progress into the dogma of the coming ideal, "scientific" society. Further, a bourgeois society, as long as it continues to believe that the good life can be built on purely commercial foundations, cannot remain seriously averse to the economic interpretation of all things. And finally, an uncurbed and undirected technology threatens to mechanize more and more areas of life, until at last the human being retires in favor of the stereotyped mass man, and the human community gives place to the "scientific" collective.[11]

Why is it that modern civilization which, all along, has been distinguished by its humanism, its glorification of man, and its preoccupation with the ideal society, turns out in the end to be antihuman and destructive of both the human person and the human community? The root of the trouble is the failure of modern thought to understand man and the human situation in all the fullness of their being. And behind this misunderstanding lies the erroneous conviction that science is the key of knowledge which by itself can exhaustively explain the nature of man and finally solve the human problem.

Modern thought has taken shape under the influence of the "scientific" tradition. This climate of opinion or frame of reference is made up of assumptions which are illicit generalizations of the working and limiting principles of science proper.

# CHART: Representing the Relationship Between Western Thought and Society and Marxist Communism and Totalitarianism

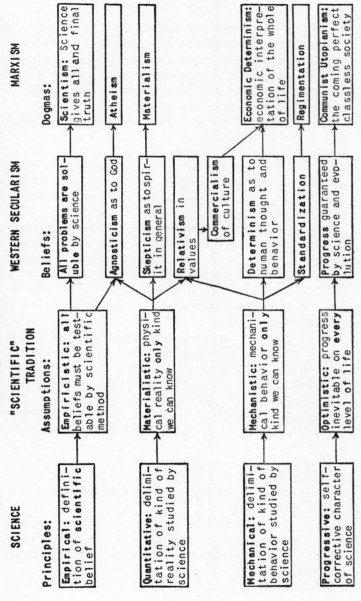

| SCIENCE | "SCIENTIFIC" TRADITION | WESTERN SECULARISM | MARXISM |
|---------|------------------------|--------------------|---------|
| **Principles:** | **Assumptions:** | **Beliefs:** | **Dogmas:** |

**Empirical:** definition of scientific belief → **Empiricistic:** all beliefs must be testable by scientific method → All problems are soluble by science → **Scientism:** Science gives all and final truth

→ Agnosticism as to God → Atheism

**Quantitative:** delimitation of kind of reality studied by science → **Materialistic:** physical reality only kind we can know → Skepticism as to spirit in general → Materialism

→ Relativism in values → Commercialism of culture

**Mechanical:** delimitation of kind of behavior studied by science → **Mechanistic:** mechanical behavior only kind we can know → Determinism as to human thought and behavior → **Economic Determinism:** economic interpretation of the whole of life

→ Standardization → Regimentation

**Progressive:** self-corrective character of science → **Optimistic:** progress inevitable on every level of life → Progress guaranteed by science and evolution → **Communist Utopianism:** the coming perfect classless society

The empirical, quantitative, mechanical, and progressive principles become the empiricistic, materialistic, mechanistic, and optimistic axioms. On the basis of these biases and presuppositions, modern thought has developed along three main lines, each of which when put into practice has fatal results for the human being and his society.

First of all, there is materialistic scientism, which places its main hopes on the social sciences. Interpreting the human situation in terms of the axioms of the " scientific " intellectual atmosphere, it inevitably arrives at materialistic, deterministic, and utopian dogmas. The result, in practice, is not a genuine society but an economic collective, and not real people but economic units.

The second version of scientism is naturalistic in character. It puts its central faith in the science of psychology. Analyzing man on the basis of the same presuppositions, it explains his essence and behavior entirely in terms of natural instincts. The result on the social level is Nazi barbarism, and on the human level, the " faceless " men who are mere pulses in the racial blood stream.

Finally, there is empirical scientism which thinks that science in general is the all-sufficient key of knowledge. Under the influence of the same set of axioms, it produces a secularized culture which is agnostic, relativistic, commercial, standardized, and, in the end, thoroughly skeptical. Its society is individualistic, bourgeois capitalism, and its inhabitants are " hollow " men whose lives are without meaning or hope. Since this condition is intolerable, what may easily happen is that the tendencies that Western secularism shares with other forms of scientism may be taken farther forward to produce a " scientific " mass society, which will differ only in name from Communist collectivism.

These are the various rooms into which they enter who believe that science, in one or all of its varieties, is the sole sufficient key of knowledge which will open the door to human salvation.

# CONCLUSION

•

# 11

## Science, Man, and Religion

•

THE CHIEF WEAKNESS OF THE
" scientific " tradition and the various forms of scientism is a
failure to understand the depths and heights of human nature
itself. Science, which man invented, cannot understand man;
for man is a person and science is equipped to handle only the
impersonal.

When the scientific method, with its quantitative and mechanical principles, is turned upon the human being, it is
bound to interpret him in impersonal terms, either as the focus
of his economic relationships (Marxism) or as a set of natural
instincts (Freudianism) or as just a clever animal (Darwinism). Man is all these things. But if we say that he is *nothing
but* an economic and instinctual animal, we commit the fallacy
of reduction. We fail to see that the scientific picture, owing
to the limitations of the scientific camera, is always partial and
incomplete.

Because of the nature of its method, science is limited to observations of the quantitative; it cannot see the human spirit.
Because of the nature of its aim, which is to formulate general
laws, it is restricted to the study of mechanical behavior; it
cannot deal with freedom. For the same reasons, it must remain
blind to the reality of human values and to the necessity of human religion. The genuine scientist will conclude that, as a
scientist, he is incapable of discussing these questions which,
as a human being, he must not disregard. It is only the pseudo
scientist, the scientolator, the exponent of scientism, who goes

173

on to insist that there is no spirit, no freedom, and that values and religion are illusions.

To deny the genuine reality of these factors, however, is to deprive man of his real humanity. And when these denials are put into practice, in contemporary totalitarianism, human personality is clearly destroyed and the possibility of human community precluded. The paradox and tragedy of the present situation in the democratic West is that while it strenuously resists this fate in the shape of Communism, it has itself abandoned its own rich literary, philosophical, and religious inheritance in favor of a meager " scientific " secularism, which must eventually either evaporate into a nerveless skepticism or else petrify into the dogmas that have produced the thing it hates.

The hope of modern democracy resides in the fact that its roots reach down to a tradition that is older and wiser than the " scientific." Behind and underneath our Western civilization lie the insights of the ancient Greeks, the Hebrews, the early and medieval Christians. It was on this foundation that science and democracy themselves were built. We have not altogether lost our hold upon this wisdom from the past; and it is for this reason that, in spite of all the teachings of naturalism, determinism, relativism, and agnosticism, we nevertheless retain our faith in the free, responsible human spirit; in the reality of goodness, beauty, truth, and justice; and in the principles of religion. These beliefs must be revived and deepened if the Western world is to be rescued from the fate that seems to be reserved for a " scientific " age.

## Science and Man

How did it happen that the " scientific " age began to doubt the reality of spirit and freedom, in which our Western civilization had all along so strongly believed? The answer is that science, which was its guiding star, is capable of dealing only with objects, things, nature; it has to treat everything that it studies, including man, as though it belonged to this category. Now it is true that man is an object, a thing, and a part of nature. His economic needs, his instinctual drives, and his animality are real and important aspects of his being. Science has, therefore, contributed enormously to our understanding of ourselves, and this new knowledge must never be abandoned in favor of a false " spiritual " and idealistic anthropology. On the other hand, we must always insist, against the reductions of scientism, that man is not only an object, *but also a subject*. It is precisely to this fact that we refer when we say that man is not just a thing but also a person, and that he belongs not only to the order of nature but also to the order of spirit.

As soon as we have made this distinction, we may be suspected of departmentalizing human nature. We do in fact suggest that in analyzing man it is necessary to distinguish clearly between the various aspects of his being: the physical, which is studied by the physical sciences; the psychical, which is investigated by psychology; and the spiritual, about which science can tell us nothing. But these are simply aspects of human nature, which are distinguishable in analysis, not parts, which are separated in fact. The distinctions themselves, therefore, cannot be drawn in any absolute and final form. Body, soul, and spirit, taken by themselves, are abstractions, and not real, independent entities. To suppose that they are different " things " is to commit what A. N. Whitehead has labeled the fallacy of " misplaced concreteness."

Man is not a sum of three parts, nor a box with three compartments. He is an organic whole, in which distinct but closely interrelated and interdependent aspects may be isolated for certain purposes. Thus the science of medicine isolates the physical and treats the body as an object; and the science of psychology isolates the psychical and treats the soul as an object. But it is highly significant that the comparatively new science of psychosomatic medicine has learned that both these " objects " are more or less artificial abstractions and that neither can be understood or treated apart from the other. Similarly when we insist that man is not only a psychosomatic object but also a spiritual subject, we must be careful to emphasize that the spirit is *not* a third " part " which can be investigated and cultivated without regard for the rest of his being.

At the same time, just as the psyche has to be distinguished from the body, so the spirit, which is known on the deepest levels of experience as the essential self, has to be distinguished from the psyche or soul, which is known to the science of psychology as a set of natural quasibiological functions. The essential difference between the psyche and the spirit is this: The psyche, in abstraction, can be considered, like the body, *as an object or thing;* it can be objectified and studied as a part of nature. The human spirit, on the other hand, can *never be considered as an object;* it can never be objectified because it can never be either observed, like the body, or introspected, like the psyche; it cannot be observed because it is always that which is doing the observing; it cannot be introspected because it is always that which is carrying on the introspection. In other words, the spirit is *essentially subject;* it is never an " it," but always, in the most profound sense, the " I."

This analysis also indicates the way in which both determinism and freedom play their part in human nature. As body and psyche, man belongs to the realm of objects, things, nature, which is the realm of necessity and nonfreedom; naturalistic, sociological, and psychological determinism is, therefore, true; but it is not the whole truth. For man, as an " I," belongs also to the dimension of subjects, persons, spirit, which is the level of responsibility and freedom.

Once again, however, it would be a mistake to develop on this basis a neo-Cartesian dualism which would draw a line between the mechanical psychosomatic organism on the one hand and the free spirit on the other. When a man acts freely, he does so, not by exercising some separate faculty such as the will, nor by virtue of some independent part of his nature such as his spirit, but rather because of his spiritual status as a person. He can act with genuine freedom because he is a subject and not merely an object. And when he so acts, he does not negate or set aside the mechanisms of his body and his psyche, but *uses and directs* them in accordance with his deliberate decisions. In fact, if his decisions are to be made effective, he has to rely on the automatic functioning of the determined areas of his nature, just as the driver is dependent on the mechanical efficiency of his motor car. What happens when a man performs a free act is that he, the subject, gathers all his energies to choose some end, and the whole psychosomatic apparatus perfectly subserves his purpose.

A free human act is not arbitrary or capricious; it is an action in pursuit of some end or purpose that the agent regards as *good*. This evaluating tendency in man introduces the question of values. Man is the kind of being who recognizes that there are certain norms that ought to govern his thought and his behavior. His behavior, then, when it is specifically human and not merely a relapse to the animal level, is not only free but also purposeful and valuational. In the field of values, the sciences, especially the social and psychological, have again made important contributions. They have exposed the nonrational and impersonal forces that too often *impose* upon us our standard of values and determine for us our conception of what is good.

It is necessary to understand that those norms which are thus unconsciously thrust upon us, in the first place are entirely relative to the particular social and psychological conditions that produced them, and in the second place are enslaving and corrupting in their effects on the human personality. We take over too easily the accepted standards of our environment and then proceed to give these relative comprehensions of truth, justice, and goodness an absolute and eternal status. We then become tied and bound to these false absolutes in a way that is psychologically unwholesome, if not disastrous.

This fact has long been understood precisely by those who are concerned to expound and defend the true values of life. The New Testament, for instance, contains some well-known attacks on moral self-righteousness and legalism. The Christian philosopher Berdyaev has pointed out that

" the slavery of man to himself is not only slavery to his lower animal nature. . . . Man becomes a slave also to his higher nature. . . . He turns the highest values into instruments of egocentric self-affirmation. . . . The typical Pharisee is the type of man in whom

devotion to the law of goodness and purity . . . has been turned
into . . . self-satisfaction. . . . This means the setting up of idols
and a false relation to ideas. . . ." [1]

Rigid adherence to our own moral laws, as though they fully
embraced the highest values, can easily degenerate into bondage and idol worship. St. Thomas Aquinas put the same point
in a different way:

" If we consider the act of will as inclined towards a seeming good,
a man acts freely when he follows the passion . . . but he acts
slavishly if, while his will remains the same, he refrains from what
he desires through fear of the [moral] law which forbids the fulfillment of the desire." [2]

If a man refrains from doing what he wants to do simply and
solely out of irrational obedience to some ethical standard of
society, then he is in bondage to that law, and all that modern
psychology has to say about the baneful influence of such
" morality " is true.

The fact that such writers as these can speak in language
that is so similar to that of Freud suggests that a recognition of
the truth contained in the sociological and psychological analyses of values does not necessarily entail the thoroughgoing relativism that is advocated by scientism as the final solution of
the whole question. In fact, if there were no objective values
denoted by the terms " true " and " good," then all human activity, including the whole scientific enterprise itself, would
be pointless and inexplicable. Every human act aims at something which the agent regards as " good," and every human assertion, including the assertion of relativism, aims at being
" true." The modern sciences of man have exposed the extent
to which our conceptions of what is " good " and " true " are
determined by irrational and extraneous forces. Certainly, therefore, their claim to objectivity needs careful scrutiny. But underlying this exposure itself is the tacit assumption that the
exposure *ought* to be made, both in the interests of *the objective truth* and also because all human behavior ought to aim at
what is *objectively good*.

Every human being, as such, implicitly believes — and this

is most obvious precisely in the utopianism of scientolators like Marx and Freud — that there is a true end, a genuine, objective, and highest good, in the pursuit of which man's conduct becomes right, his thought true, and his life meaningful.

## Science and Religion

Under the influence of the " scientific " tradition, we have tended to assume that the proper way to arrive at a full knowledge of the whole of reality, including man himself, is through the study of external objects and of nonhuman nature. An older procedure was to begin with man, and from the clues discovered in this way to go on to interpret the rest of reality, including the physical world. If the latter method is open to the danger of the " pathetic " fallacy, which endows inanimate nature with human feelings, the former is just as liable to the " apathetic " fallacy, which supposes that the human being can be completely understood in terms appropriate to nature.

As between these two procedures, one thing is certain: the one kind of reality that we know, so to speak, *from the inside*, is man; we know nature only from the outside. We know what it is like to be a man; we do not know what it is like to be a planet. " Know thyself," was the maxim that Socrates, very early in the history of reflective thought, adopted as his starting point. And if, unprejudiced by the assumptions of the " scientific " climate of opinion, we consult the plain facts of self-knowledge, we shall begin our search for understanding with an indubitable conviction of the reality of spirit, freedom, and values.

This is also the only path to that understanding of human life, both in the individual and in society, which is what we mean by wisdom. It is the sympathetic insight, based on an identity between ourselves and what we study — quite different from the external knowledge of science — which enables us to enter into the inner being of our fellows. Certainly we can know them, scientifically, by observing how they act as objects; but we can never truly understand them unless we appreciate their inner aims and motives, and the values that move them as subjects. "We always understand more than we know." [3]

These last words are borrowed from the German sociologist and philosopher Wilhelm Dilthey, who was intensely concerned with the question: "How do we understand other human beings? how do we enter into and appreciate their motives?" We do so, he said, by studying the various ways in which they *express* themselves. We cannot properly understand even our own thoughts and feelings until we put them into words. Obviously, therefore, we shall be unable really to appreciate others — individuals, societies, and civilizations — until, on the basis of self-knowledge and identification, we study and interpret their various modes of self-expression.

The primary medium of expression is literature and art. It is here that we find the depths of human nature and the inner realities of human existence communicated with a vivacity and richness that scientific analysis can never match. We shall never understand the reaches of human life until we have seen it through the eyes of a Homer, a Euripides, or a Shakespeare. It is familiarity with the great expressions of the human spirit that deepens man's wisdom and his insights into human nature, and that heightens his vision of greatness and his awareness of what is really good — and bad.

The humanities alone, of course, cannot convey a complete comprehension of life. The sciences are equally necessary. The latter have to do with the natural context, the material conditions and machinery of human life and human society. As Dilthey pointed out, the sociological and psychological study of the background of a Goethe is essential to a full appreciation of what he wrote. These factors are not, as scientism would have us believe, the sufficient explanation of his works, but they are the material conditions within which his thought developed; they are, therefore, not, as some would say, entirely irrelevant. Full understanding of life requires both humane wisdom and scientific knowledge.

The sciences of man are too apt to disregard the data provided by the humanities. In the first place, therefore, the specifically human experiences of joy, grief, love, despair, faith, and sacrifice are either not dealt with at all or are treated in an unbalanced and inadequate fashion. In the second place, the social worker or psychologist, who is trained in science but ignorant of the world's great literature, is well equipped with techniques but lacking in insights, full of knowledge but devoid of wisdom. He is apt to be a mere technician who manipulates; and the tragedy is that he manipulates, not things where control is appropriate, but human beings where manipulation is fatal. If he is to help his fellow men, at the most crucial points, he must relate his knowledge to wisdom.

On the other hand, he who is steeped in the humanities and inspired with passionate sympathy, but lacks all scientific knowledge of the part that is played in human life by instincts and social pressures, has his feet firmly planted in mid-air. If he is to be of any assistance to others, he needs to be brought down to earth and to relate his wisdom to knowledge.

In addition to the world's great literature, another and even more profound source of wisdom is religion. The literary and religious approach to understanding is the same. In both cases, the clues to the ultimate understanding of all things are derived, not from external nature, as in scientism, but from the internal nature of man. If it is a question of the nature of being as such, this being, our own human being, is the being that we know most intimately. Now the essence of this human being is free, personal, value-seeking spirit. Since this is the nature of being where we know it most nearly and from the inside, is it not reasonable, says the religious man, to conclude that the highest reality is also free, personal, purposeful spirit, the primary and transcendent Subject, the " I Am that I Am " who is God?

As far as the nature of ultimate reality is concerned, we are in the realm of faith no matter what our beliefs may be. But the wisdom that belongs to art and religion seems to dig deeper into the nature of things than the knowledge of science, which must stop with the things of nature.

Again, however, as in the case of our understanding of man and of human values, we must not be unmindful of the contributions that science itself has made to the cause of true religion. Religious beliefs and practices have frequently been misdirected and vitiated by prescientific ignorance of, and bondage to, the forces not only of nature but also of society and the psyche. Scientific knowledge puts an end to this superstition and idolatry. The social sciences discover that primitive worship, and much that still masquerades as religion, is actually directed partly at deified natural powers and partly at apotheosized social patterns. Similarly, psychological investigations reveal that the idea of God is often merely the projection of subjective psychical conditions. True religion welcomes these exposures. For if natural forces, social structures, or psychological projections are mistaken for the divine, their worship is idolatry and their service is enslavement. The scientific study of religion releases us from bondage to false gods and makes possible a free, conscious deliberate decision either for or against the true God — whose service is perfect freedom.

Science and religion have frequently appeared to be in conflict and it has been falsely assumed, on both sides of the controversy, that science is necessarily inimical to religious belief. In actual fact, of course, it is scientism and not science that militates against religion. On the one hand, the champions of religion have tended to confuse these two very different things and to attack the theories of science when they should have been opposing the dogmas of scientism. On the other hand, religion has often been attacked in the name of science by those who were really serving the cause of scientism. In the former case, we can speak of the conflict between pseudo religion and genuine science, and in the latter of the strife between pseudo science and genuine religion. In addition it may have happened that pseudo science and pseudo religion have sometimes locked horns in spurious battle. But the one thing that is certain is that true religion and true science have always fought on the same side.

In the seventeenth century some religious people regarded the Newtonian system as atheistic, in the sense that it drove God out of nature. Everything could now be explained by

means of the laws of motion and the hypothesis of God became
unnecessary. What these critics failed to understand was that
Newton was looking at nature through scientific spectacles and
faithfully describing what he saw; his view was correct within
the limits imposed by the nature of his lenses. It is also possible to look at nature through artistic or religious spectacles,
and the view that one gets is very different. There can be no
conflict, however, as long as we admit that what the scientific,
the artistic, or the religious genius sees is actually present and
that the differences are due to different perspectives. The trouble begins when one party insists that his spectacles are the
only ones that give the objective truth. The defenders of religion who made this mistake in regard to Newtonian physics were victims of pseudo religion. At the same time, there
were those, like the philosopher Hobbes, who attempted to
turn the theories of science into the whole and final truth about
reality in general. This was materialistic scientism, the product
not of science but of pseudo science.

Again, in the nineteenth century, when Darwin published his
theory of evolution, there were those who claimed at once that
the hypothesis must be false since it contradicted the Biblical
story of creation. They thought that since the Biblical and the
scientific accounts were talking about more or less the same
thing in apparently quite different ways, they could not both
be true. Such a conclusion involved, of course, a tacit reduction of the profoundly wise and beautiful story in Genesis to
the same level as a scientific description. Failing to understand
that it is possible to look at the same thing from different points
of view, these people opposed a genuine scientific theory in the
interests of pseudo religion.

Examples of apparent conflict between science and religion
that are more contemporary come from the human sciences.
These sciences tend to take over uncritically the presuppositions of the " scientific " tradition, instead of recognizing the
limitations involved in adherence to the principles of science.
They therefore tend to lapse into pseudo science and to deny
the reality of God, spirit, freedom, and values. On the other

hand, in their authentic scientific capacity, they have made invaluable discoveries about man and his society, which pseudo religion noisily attacks.

The right way in which religion should criticize scientific sociology is to point out that it looks at human society through the limiting lenses of the scientific spectacles, and is therefore restricted in its view to the material and impersonally determining factors in social history. If it proceeds to assert that these factors constitute the whole social reality, it ceases to be science and becomes scientism. For there are, in fact, a host of other essential factors at work in history, above all the purposes of God and the spirit and freedom of man. When religion speaks in this way against the dogmas of pseudoscientific sociology, it is the voice of genuine religion challenging the illegitimate assertions of an economic materialism, which, it should be remembered, is widely preached today even in non-Marxist sociological circles.

The wrong way in which to launch an attack on economic determinism and cultural relativism is to refuse to admit the important role that material factors play in shaping social organization and individual character. To ignore or deny this fact is the mark of an idealistic pseudo religion, which is here in conflict with a well-substantiated sociological theory. We even have to recognize that the operative motive in the defense of religion is often an unconscious awareness of its usefulness in preserving the *status quo* and in protecting the material interests of a privileged class against threatening revolutionary movements.

There are also two ways in which religion can react to the findings of scientific psychology. The right way is to admit the truth of scientific analyses as valid descriptions of the limited view of human nature which is all that is possible for the scientific method. Part of the truth about man is that he is constituted by instincts which largely determine his behavior, and that the particular forms that his norms and standards take are relative to certain social and psychological circumstances. It is pseudo science, however, and not science, that draws the illegitimate conclusion that this is the whole truth about human nature, conduct, and values. Similarly, it is true that the idea of God, in some cases, has its origin and character correctly explained in Freudian terms, but this fact by no means proves that belief in God is illusory. Finally, it is undoubtedly the case that psychological techniques are capable of benefiting those areas of human being with which they are equipped to deal. At the same time, the science of psychology remains blind to the profundities of the human spirit, and in these deep places, where the crucial issues are joined, a greater wisdom must be summoned to man's aid.

The wrong way in which religion is tempted to criticize the discoveries of modern psychology is to deny altogether the truth of its weightily confirmed hypotheses. There is in some quarters a tendency to reject the reality and power of the animal part of man's nature, the conventional and repressive elements in man-made moral laws, and the degree to which scientific therapy can assist in the cure of souls. Such an attitude is the obscurantism of pseudo religion confronting the findings of genuine science.

Both scientific sociology and scientific psychology add greatly to our knowledge and control of the human situation. It is only when the exponents of these sciences lapse into scientism, and advance the limiting principles of science as though they were universal truths which can exhaustively explain and solve all human problems, that the representatives of religion must stand in implacable and aggressive opposition.

Pseudo science is the characteristic aberration of a " scientific " age; it transforms the valid principles of science into general assumptions that have definite antireligious implications. Pseudo religion, for its part, confuses science and scientism and, when it should be resisting the latter, actually attacks the former; this procedure inevitably creates the impression that religion is antiscientific. An examination of the actual conflicts that have been thought to exist between science and religion shows that in every case the quarrel was either between pseudo science and genuine religion or between pseudo religion and genuine science. True science and true religion never come to blows but always co-operate in the education of mankind.

## Science and the Christian Faith

If science and religion are both necessary for a full understanding of life and reality, the essential requirement of the present day is the construction of a synthesis between the findings of modern science and the older truths of religion. This is the only way in which religion, on the one hand, can be prevented from withdrawing into idealism and otherworldliness, and the " scientific " age, on the other hand, can be rescued from ruin in antihuman collectivism.

The reconciliation of science and religion is only possible, for several reasons, in terms of the Christian faith. In the first place, the modern " scientific " tradition has roots in the Christian tradition of the medieval period. Just as there was no abrupt break between the new age and its predecessor, so the new tradition grew out of, and to some extent on the shoulders of, the old. It may be, then, that our " scientific " civilization can be redeemed by reincorporation into the Christian context out of which it sprang.

In the second place, Christianity, with its realistic, thisworldly emphases, is the one great religion that can appeal to the new age now struggling to be born; for that age, it is hoped, will wish neither to turn its back on science, in the fashion of otherworldly religions, nor to be content with science by itself, in the fashion of scientism.

Thirdly, the four basic theses of the " scientific " tradition are closely related to certain essential Christian doctrines, which they serve to illuminate and reinforce. The four theses are empiricism, materialism, determinism, and optimism. The connection between these four doctrines and the corresponding articles of the Christian faith can be only briefly traced here, so as merely to suggest a possible synthesis that might inspire a new tradition for the new age.

Empiricism means devotion to the scientific method. This method of gaining knowledge was largely neglected in the medieval age, and consequently there was virtually no material progress throughout that period. The outstanding characteristic of the modern age, on the contrary, is the vast increase in knowledge and power which is due precisely to the scientific method. In the Christian view, the power that science has put into the hands of men is part of the purpose of God for the human race. In the very first chapter of the Bible we are told that God said, " Let them have dominion . . . over all the earth." [4] It is only in the last four centuries that this " dominion " has increasingly become a reality.

In prescientific ages man, far from being the master of his environment, was more or less the slave, not only of natural forces, but also of social structures and psychical mechanisms. Again according to the Bible, when God's purpose was republished and farther advanced in the revealing and redemptive work of Christ, man was released from this " bondage under the elements of the world." [5] The various sciences have clearly played their part in this cosmic plan of redemption: the natural sciences have liberated men from bondage to nature, the social sciences from bondage to society, and psychology from bondage to their own psyches. And the Christian must recognize that this release through science has taken place within the purposes of God.

On the other hand the Christian religion is bound to insist that the scientific method is not the only path to understanding. In addition to the knowledge that science gives there is wisdom that comes in other ways. The notion that science can answer all questions is based on the pretentious assumption that there are no mysteries in the face of which the human reason falters, but only problems that remain for the human mind to solve. But in addition to the many soluble problems that science has still to tackle, there are also certain impenetrable mysteries which science is powerless to touch: the mystery of life itself and death, the mystery of suffering and sacrifice, the awful mystery of evil, and the no less awful mystery of loveliness. It is at the deeper levels of the spirit and of faith that these mysteries are met and penetrated.

In regard to the relationship between materialism and the Christian creed, there is Temple's famous saying that Christianity is " the most avowedly materialist of all the great religions." [6] In contrast to the otherworldly and escapist tendencies of other great religions, the Christian faith, as properly understood, has always insisted on the reality and importance of the material universe. In the first place, God made the world " and, behold, it was very good." [7] This earth especially, in the Biblical view, has an everlasting significance and an eternal place in the purposes of God.

Further, when God's plan for this planet and for its inhabitants appeared to be frustrated, then God thought that it was both possible and fit that he himself should come down into the world and take our flesh upon him. Anyone who understands the doctrine of the incarnation can never again be contemptuous of the natural order which was capable of sustaining this incursion.

The teaching of the resurrection of the body has a similar significance. It is this doctrine, and not the immortality of the soul, that expresses the Christian view of man's ultimate destiny. Man is an organic whole, in which the physical, psychical, and spiritual can be distinguished but not separated. It is this whole man, and not some disembodied spirit, who is intended for eternal life. Man, at the consummation of all things, is not to escape from his body but to have it glorified and transformed into the perfect instrument of his spirit. Similarly, at the end, man does not flee away from the earth into an ethereal sphere, but sees the earth also changed and exalted into the locale of the everlasting Kingdom. At the very end of the Bible, as at the beginning, the eternal significance of the earth and the whole material sphere is unmistakably asserted: " I saw a new heaven and a new earth: . . . I . . . saw the holy city, . . . coming down from God out of heaven." [8]

On the other side, of course, Christianity must insist, against any unadulterated materialism, that what one sees with the outward eye is not the whole reality. In addition to the realm of matter, objects, and nature, which has its permanent and essential place, there is also the dimension of spirit, subjects, and persons, which, in the last analysis has a prior and more ultimate significance.

The third main feature of the " scientific " tradition is its determinism. This doctrine contains a truth that the Christian must not only reluctantly accept but also recognize as essential to his own beliefs. According to Biblical religion, man is not in fact free but in " bondage under the elements of the world." And this bondage is recognized, in both the scientific and the Christian view, as not only the loss of freedom but also " the bondage of corruption." [9] For in so far as our standards and beliefs are not freely chosen but forced upon us by social and psychical pressures, which feed upon our lust for power and our economic and sexual selfishness, and in so far as this self-interest tempts us to raise our relative and approximate comprehensions to the level of the absolute and the eternal, to that extent our norms and principles are corrupted and our conception of the true ends of life inferior and false. This is the teaching of Marx in his doctrine of the ideological taint, and of Freud in his pansexual determinism. It is also teaching of Christianity under the concept of sin.

The Christian doctrine of sin, however, pierces to a deeper level than the various versions of scientific determinism. It recognizes, as they do not, that the lust for power and economic and sexual self-interest are simply symptoms of the underlying disease of self-centeredness. The salvation of man, therefore, lies not in an authoritarian state which can suppress the natural instincts, nor in a new economic system which will eradicate all greed, nor in psychoanalysis which reorganizes the psyche, but rather in some mighty act that can heal this radical perversion of the human spirit. For it is in the depths of man's spirit and of his essential subjectivity that his disorder has its roots. When the self turns in upon the self and self-satisfaction becomes the final end of life, then everything goes wrong. Every gain in knowledge and power, every new release from bondage, every additional acquisition of freedom — everything that science gives us — is then used in the interests of this misconceived goal and merely hurries man on the faster to his perdition. This is the truth about the human situation that accounts for the paradoxical fact that the culmination of modern progress coincides with man's imminent destruction. The awful tragedy of the situation is that once the self has become centered on the self, in this worst and most ultimate form of bondage, there is nothing that the self can do to free itself; for it is precisely the "I," the subject, at the deepest level, that needs to be redeemed.

Christians believe that the mighty act of man's redemption has been accomplished by God himself in the person of Jesus Christ who, by his *sacrifice of self* upon the cross, has opened up the way out of "the bondage of corruption into the glorious liberty of the children of God." [10] The self, which is thus freed from bondage to self, can then see that its true and highest end is to be centered on God, to grow up into a real person in the likeness of Christ, and to enter into the real community, which is his Kingdom.

This brings us to our last point. The fourth characteristic of the "scientific" age is its optimism and its belief in progress. It is this belief which, because it was founded on a secular instead of a religious hope, has been most roughly handled by the actual course of contemporary history. Nevertheless, this conviction that history is moving purposefully, that man's story on this earth has a real end and goal toward which it is proceeding, is most clearly rooted in the Christian faith. It was the Bible, first of all, that gave to men the notion that history moves meaningfully in a straight line from a beginning to an end, and not aimlessly in a circle, as the Greeks, for instance, thought. The end of history and the eternal purpose of God in creation and redemption is, in the Christian view, the establishment of his Kingdom — the community of persons related in love to one another and to God.

Marxist Communism has a secularized version of this hope. It paints a picture of the consummation of all things in the form of the ideal society of perfect justice and brotherhood which is guaranteed by the nature of things and by the historical dialectic. It maintains that the future belongs to it. This is the secret of its success among the young in heart, whose glance is always forward. Christians, meanwhile, have been too content to look to the past, which is the posture of age, and to stress the glorious inheritance which they have received from the days of old. Yet the Christian faith is the original source of the true vision of the future, the vision of the community of love, which is ordained by the promises of God and achieved by the divine dialectic.

It is techniques that the scientific age, first and foremost, has contributed to human life: techniques which can control atomic energy, build social structures, and determine psychical development. Techniques, however, are only instruments, and the crucial question is, For what ends shall we use these means? On the one hand, we can manufacture atomic bombs which can virtually destroy the world; we can construct a " scientific " society which would destroy true community; we can condition the human psyche so as to destroy personality. Scientific knowledge and power can easily be used for the ruination of the human world, the human community, and the human person.

On the other hand, atomic energy can be utilized to give men " dominion . . . over all the earth"; sociological techniques are indispensable for the production of the good society; and psychology is needed for the development of mature persons.

Everything depends on the purposes at which we aim, on the values that we cherish, and on our convictions as to what is good. And our purposes, our values, and our convictions are all, in turn, derived from our conception of the true end of life. What is this true end? The Christian faith believes that it is given to us in the twofold picture of " a perfect man, the measure of the stature of the fulness of Christ," [11] and the perfect community, the Kingdom of God, concerning which we pray daily that it may come on earth as it is in heaven.

Christ said, " I am come that they might have life, and that they might have it more abundantly." [12] The various sciences furnish us with the material conditions of the more abundant life. In the meantime, flushed with our accomplishments, we have lost sight of the goal and no longer know where we are going. In the absence of direction and purpose, our scientific knowledge, power, and freedom may be misused and bring us to disaster. But now, if we recover the beautiful, profound, and ancient wisdom of our faith, then science, under the providence of God and within his cosmic purpose of redemption, can play its appointed part in bringing us to "the haven where we would be." [13]

As always, man stands at the place of decision. The double potentialities for good and evil of the present situation simply offer to man once again, in more extreme form, the choice that he has always had to make.

•

## Notes to Chapter 1

[1] I do not mean to imply that the spirit is a third "part" of man completely distinct from the body and the psyche. The spiritual, the psychical, and the physical are not three separate entities in human nature, but rather three aspects of one organic whole. The psyche and the body are "natural" and can be studied scientifically as objects. But the spirit is always *subject* and, therefore, cannot be known in the same way. Nor should the distinction between the spiritual and the "natural" be thought of metaphysically as an ultimate dualism, but rather existentially as the difference between subject and object. These questions are discussed more fully in ch. 11 below.

[2] Heisenberg's principle of indeterminacy rules out any crude interpretation of the mechanistic analogy in relation to the physical universe. The laws of physics are now regarded as statistical rather than mechanical. Nevertheless, science is still concerned only with events that happen in regular and predictable series, and it is convenient to continue to call this kind of behavior "mechanical" as distinct from "purposive" or "free."

[3] The connections and differences between science, the "scientific" tradition, and scientism may be shown diagrammatically as follows:

| Science | Scientific Tradition | Scientism |
|---|---|---|
| Limiting principles: | General assumptions: | Universal dogmas: |
| 1. Empirical | 1. Empiricistic | 1. Science=all truth |
| 2. Quantitative | 2. Materialistic | 2. Materialism |
| 3. Mechanical | 3. Mechanistic | 3. Determinism |
| 4. Progressive | 4. Optimistic | 4. Utopianism |

## Notes to Chapter 2

[1] *The Leviathan,* T. Hobbes (Everyman's Library), chs. 1 to 3.
[2] *Ibid.,* ch. 6.
[3] *Ibid.,* p. 28.

[4] *Ibid.*, p. 49.

[5] *Ibid.*, p. 66.

[6] *Ibid.*, pp. 64, 65.

[7] *Ibid.*, chs. 17, 18.

[8] *A Discourse on the Positive Spirit*, A. Comte (William Reeves, London, 1903), p. 20.

[9] *Ibid.*, p. 78: "After the great crisis which was the starting point of modern positivity (associated with the names of Galileo, Kepler, Descartes, and Bacon) nothing was left essentially outside the scientific movement . . . except moral and social theories, which have remained since then fenced off from the domain of reason under the barren domination of the theologico-metaphysical spirit. To positivists this also is the last and, in our day, the principal task of the true philosophic spirit which has already obtained a fair footing in all the other main branches of knowledge." See also pp. 88, 89.

[10] *Positive Philosophy*, A. Comte (D. Appleton & Co., London, 1853), p. 407.

[11] *The Leviathan*, chs. 31 and 39.

[12] *Ibid.*, pp. 17, 55.

[13] *Ibid.*, pp. 54, 55.

[14] *Positive Philosophy*, pp. 15, 16.

[15] *A General View of Positivism*, A. Comte (Routledge & Sons, London, 1908), ch. 6.

## Notes to Chapter 3

[1] Max Eastman (ed.), *Capital, The Communist Manifesto, and Other Writings* (The Modern Library, New York, 1932), p. viii. Eastman, a far from sympathetic critic of Marxism, nevertheless admits, in his introduction to this collection of Marxist writings (hereafter referred to in these notes as *Capital, etc.*), that " Marx gave the world as important a gift of scientific knowledge as any man of the modern era: he is one of the giants of science."

[2] *Ibid.*, p. 10.

[3] *Ibid.*, p. xxii.

[4] *Ibid.*, pp. xxi–xxiii.

[5] *Ibid.*, p. xxii.

[6] *Ibid.*, p. xxiii.

[7] Quoted by C. E. M. Joad, *Guide to Philosophy* (Gollancz, London, 1936). p. 484.

[8] *Capital, etc.*, pp. 8, 9.

[9] *Ibid.*, p. 318. Cf. F. Engels, *Socialism: Utopian and Scientific* (International Publishers, New York, 1935), p. 51: " The economic

structure of society always furnishes the real basis, starting *from which we can alone work out the ultimate explanation* of the whole superstructure of juridical and political institutions as well as of the religious, philosophical, and other ideas of a given historical period." In both quotations, the italics are mine.

10 *Socialism: Utopian and Scientific,* p. 54.

11 See Part I of *The Communist Manifesto,* in *Capital, etc.,* pp. 321 ff.

12 *Ibid.,* p. 318.

13 *Ibid.,* p. 333.

14 *Ibid.,* pp. 318, 319.

15 *Ibid.,* p. 355.

16 *Ibid.,* p. 342.

17 *Ibid.,* p. 343.

18 *Loc. cit.*

19 *Loc. cit.*

20 K. Marx, *Critique of the Gotha Programme* (International Publishers, New York, 1938), p. 75.

21 *Capital, etc.,* p. 7.

22 *Ibid.,* quoted by Eastman in his introduction, p. xvi.

23 K. Marx, " A Criticism of the Hegelian Philosophy of Right," in *Selected Essays,* H. J. Stenning, trans. (Leonard Parsons, London, 1926), p. 12. It is possible that Marx borrowed this famous phrase from the Anglican clergyman, novelist, and radical, Charles Kingsley.

24 See p. 32 above.

25 K. Marx, " Theses on Feuerbach," in F. Engels, *Ludwig Feuerbach* (Foreign Languages Publishing House, Moscow, 1946), p. 78.

26 *Capital, etc.,* p. 342.

## Notes to Chapter 4

1 F. Engels, *Ludwig Feuerbach,* p. 25.

2 On man as spirit as well as part of nature, see note 1 to ch. 1 above, and ch. 11 below.

3 The Freudian analysis of man is fully dealt with in ch. 6 below.

4 " Self-interest in general " is, of course, what Christianity means by " sin "; see ch. 11 below.

5 See, e.g., R. R. Marett, *The Threshold of Religion* (Methuen and Company, London, 1929), and R. Otto, *The Idea of the Holy* (Oxford University Press, London, 1923).

6 A. J. Toynbee, *A Study of History* (Abridgment by D. C. Somervell, Oxford University Press, London, 1946), p. 60.

## Notes to Chapter 5

[1] The terms " hard " and " soft " in this connection are borrowed from Irving Babbit, *Rousseau and Romanticism* (Houghton Mifflin Company, Cambridge, Mass., 1919).

[2] J. J. Rousseau, " A Discourse on the Origin of Inequality," in *The Social Contract and Discourses* (Everyman's Library, London, 1913), p. 181.

[3] *Petits Chefs d'Oeuvre* (Firmin-Didot, Paris, 1876), pp. 503 ff.

[4] *Loc. cit.*

[5] *The Social Contract*, I, I.

[6] Both essays are contained in the Everyman volume.

[7] *The Social Contract*, I, VI.

[8] " Discourse on Political Science," in the Everyman volume, p. 253.

[9] *The Social Contract*, II, III.

[10] *Ibid.*, I, VII.

[11] *Ibid.*, I, VIII.

[12] " Discourse on Political Economy," in the Everyman volume, p. 263.

[13] *Ibid.*, p. 268.

[14] Quoted by G. H. Sabine, *A History of Political Theory* (Henry Holt and Company, Inc., New York, 1937), p. 591.

[15] *Rousseau and Romanticism*, p. 345.

[16] See ch. 8, below.

[17] Quoted by Engels, *Socialism: Utopian and Scientific* (International Publishers, New York, 1935), p. 12.

[18] See W. B. Chamberlain, *Heaven Wasn't His Destination* (Allen & Unwin, London, 1941), p. 150.

[19] L. Feuerbach, *The Essence of Christianity* (Trans. George Eliot, Houghton Mifflin Company, Boston, 1881), p. 197.

[20] *Ibid.;* see chs. 2 and 3 above.

[21] Cf. F. Von Hugel, *Essays and Addresses*, First Series (J. M. Dent & Sons, London, 1928), pp. 37, 38, which puts the paradox roughly as follows: The same content which, when seen in its " true " character, leaves men cold, becomes, when seen in its " false " character, the most powerful force known to history.

## Notes to Chapter 6

[1] *A General Introduction to Psycho-Analysis* (The Garden City Publishing Co., Inc., New York, 1938), p. 24.

[2] " Any such constitution as I have assumed in order to account

for neurotic symptoms can only be of universal validity." *Ibid.*, p. 261; see also pp. 397, 398.

³ *Beyond the Pleasure Principle* (Boni & Liveright, New York, 1922), p. 2. Italics mine.

⁴ *General Introduction,* p. 311. Italics mine.

⁵ " In every way analogous to hunger, *libido* is the force by means of which . . . the sexual instinct . . . achieves expression." *Ibid.,* p. 274.

⁶ *Ibid.,* p. 311.

⁷ *Beyond the Pleasure Principle,* p. 67.

⁸ *Ibid.,* pp. 67, 68. But note how this passage continues: " The conclusion that therefore there are no other instincts is one to which we do not assent." See next section of this chapter for Freud's final position on this question.

⁹ *General Introduction,* p. 246.

¹⁰ *The Ego and the Id* (Hogarth Press, London, 1927), pp. 39, 40.

¹¹ *General Introduction,* p. 296.

¹² *The Ego and the Id,* p. 31.

¹³ *Ibid.,* p. 39.

¹⁴ *Ibid.,* pp. 82, 83.

¹⁵ *Ibid.,* p. 27.

¹⁶ *The Future of an Illusion* (Hogarth Press, London, 1928), p. 81.

¹⁷ *General Introduction,* p. 395.

¹⁸ *Loc. cit.*

¹⁹ *Ibid.,* p. 396.

²⁰ *The Ego and the Id,* p. 63.

²¹ *Ibid.,* p. 55.

²² *Loc. cit.* See also *Beyond the Pleasure Principle,* pp. 46, 47: " All organic instincts are conservative . . . and are directed towards regression, towards reinstatement of something earlier . . . It would be counter to the conservative nature of instinct if the goal of life were a state never hitherto reached. It must rather be an ancient starting point which the living being left long ago, and to which it harks back again by all the circuitous paths of development . . . Everything living dies from causes within itself and returns to the inorganic; we can only say that ' the goal of all life is death.' "

²³ *Beyond the Pleasure Principle,* p. 69.

²⁴ *The Ego and the Id,* p. 56.

²⁵ *Ibid.,* p. 47.

My colleague, Professor C. R. Feilding, has pointed out to me that the word " id " is presumably the contribution of Freud's English translator, since the German is regularly *das Es.*

[26] *Ibid.,* p. 46.

[27] *Ibid.,* p. 82.

[28] See *General Introduction,* p. 310: " It is unquestionable that the course of the prescribed development in each individual can be disturbed and altered by current impressions from without. But the power which has enforced this development upon mankind and still to-day maintains its pressure in the same course, is known to us; it is, again, the frustration exacted by reality; or, if we give it its great real name, it is *necessity,* the struggle for life, ἀνάγκη." Italics Freud's.

[29] *The Ego and the Id,* p. 82.

[30] *The Basic Writings of Sigmund Freud* (ed. A. A. Brill, Modern Library, Inc., New York, 1938), p. 161.

[31] *Ibid.,* p. 162.

[32] *Civilization and Its Discontents* (Hogarth Press, London, 1930), p. 62. See also *General Introduction,* pp. 23, 24: " We believe that civilization has been built up, under the pressure of the struggle for existence, by sacrifices in gratification of the primitive impulses . . . The sexual are among the most important of the instinctive forces thus utilized."

[33] Freud, therefore, says that he has to make " exactly the same objections . . . against . . . the cultural superego " as against the individual superego; *Civilization and Its Discontents,* p. 139; see also p. 141: " Many systems of civilization − . . . possibly even the whole of humanity − have become ' neurotic ' under the pressure of the civilizing trends."

[34] *The Future of an Illusion,* p. 76.

[35] *The Ego and the Id,* p. 49.

[36] *Ibid.,* p. 45.

[37] *Civilization and Its Discontents,* p. 44.

[38] Freud's description of the " state of nature " is very like Hobbes's: " If we imagined society's prohibitions removed, then one could choose any woman who took one's fancy . . . , one could kill without hesitation one's rival . . . and one could seize what one wanted of another man's goods without asking his leave: how splendid, what a succession of delights, life would be. True, one soon finds the first difficulty: everyone else has exactly the same wishes, and will treat one with no more consideration than one will treat him . . . It is true that nature does not ask us to restrain our instincts, she lets us do as we like; but she has her peculiarly effective way of restraining us: she destroys us, coldly, cruelly, callously, as it seems to us, and possibly just through what has caused our satisfaction." *The Future of an Illusion,* pp. 25, 26.

[39] *Ibid.*, p. 69.
[40] *Ibid.*, p. 73.
[41] *Ibid.*, pp. 70 ff.
[42] *Ibid.*, pp. 79 ff.
[43] *Loc. cit.* Cf. Rousseau's "Man is naturally good and only by institutions are men made bad."
[44] *Ibid.*, p. 83.
[45] *Ibid.*, p. 93.
[46] *Ibid.*, pp. 91, 92.
[47] *Ibid.*, pp. 83, 84.
[48] *Ibid.*, pp. 69, 12–14.
[49] *Ibid.*, p. 89.
[50] *Basic Writings*, p. 32.
[51] *A Study of History*, p. 447.

## Notes to Chapter 7

[1] *Beyond the Pleasure Principle*, p. 83.
[2] *The Future of an Illusion*, p. 98. See pp. 95 ff. for Freud's hymn of praise to science.
[3] *General Introduction*, pp. 262, 263. Italics mine.
[4] It might be argued that the strongest evidence for the truth of the diagnosis is really the cure which follows. Psychoanalysis is, of course, frequently successful. But psychiatrists who operate on the basis of quite different theories, as well as many whose approach to human problems is not "scientific" at all, are often just as successful.
[5] *Mind, Medicine, and Man* (Harcourt, Brace and Company, New York, 1943), p. 333.
[6] Again this should not be taken to imply an ultimate dualism between "spirit," conceived as a separate entity, and the natural "psyche." By themselves, both are abstractions from the whole man. See note 1 to ch. 1, above, and ch. 11, below.
[7] *The Ego and the Id*, pp. 28, 29.
[8] *Ibid.*, p. 72, footnote.
[9] *Mind, Medicine, and Man*, p. 333. For a positive treatment of freedom along these lines, see ch. 11, below.
[10] *An Essay on Man* (Yale University Press, New Haven, 1944), p. 21.
[11] *Civilization and Its Discontents*, p. 143.
[12] See ch. 9, below.
[13] *The Future of an Illusion*, p. 93.
[14] *Ibid.*, pp. 11, 12. Brackets inserted.

[15] *Civilization and Its Discontents*, p. 88.

[16] *Ibid.*, p. 57.

[17] *Loc. cit.*

[18] *Loc. cit.*

[19] See ch. 8, below.

[20] In one place, and one place only as far as I can discover, Freud admitted, rather grudgingly, that the way in which a belief arises psychologically does not destroy its validity theoretically: " this does not precisely imply a refutation of religion ": *New Introductory Lectures on Psycho-Analysis* (W. W. Norton & Company, Inc., New York, 1933), p. 229. Erich Fromm, who belongs to the contemporary school of depth psychology, emphasizes this point, while himself remaining, to all intents and purposes, an atheist: *Escape from Freedom* (Farrar & Rinehart, Inc., New York, 1941), pp. 63, 64.

## Notes to Chapter 8

[1] *Novum Organum* (Colonial Press, London, 1899), p. 315.

[2] *Ibid.*, p. 366.

[3] *Essay Concerning Human Understanding*, II, VIII, 7 ff.

[4] *Ibid.*, II, XXIII, I ff.

[5] *Ibid.*, II, XXVI.

[6] *Ibid.*, IV, II, 14.

[7] *The Treatise of Human Understanding*, IV, II.

[8] *Ibid.*, I, III.

[9] *Ibid.*, I, IV, VII.

[10] See ch. 9, § I, below.

[11] *The Descent of Man*, I, III.

[12] *Ibid.*, I, IV.

[13] *Essay Concerning Human Understanding*, IV, XIX, 14.

[14] *Enquiry Concerning Human Understanding*, X.

[15] *Ibid.*, XI.

[16] We are apt to suppose that widespread religious skepticism is a more or less contemporary phenomenon. The following quotation, taken from Joseph Butler's preface to *The Analogy of Religion*, written in 1736, suggests that this supposition is erroneous: " It is come, I know not how, to be taken for granted by many persons that Christianity . . . is now at length discovered to be fictitious. And accordingly they treat it as if, in the present age, this was an agreed point among all people of discernment, and nothing remained but to set it up as a principal subject for mirth and ridicule, as it were by way of reprisal for its having so long interrupted the pleasures of the world."

[17] *Human Destiny* (Longmans, Green & Co., New York, 1947), pp. 28 ff.

## Notes to Chapter 9

[1] J. S. Mill, *Utilitarianism* (Everyman's Library, London, 1910), p. 36.

[2] *Ibid.*, p. 6.

[3] *The Meaning of Truth* (Longmans, Green & Co., Inc., New York, 1914), p. vii.

[4] According to this theory the propositions of logic and mathematics are significant and important though not empirical. They are analytical propositions which are true a priori. They are absolutely true precisely because they say nothing about experience; they are stipulations or rules for the formation and transformation of propositions.

[5] *Three Essays on Religion* (Henry Holt and Company, Inc., New York, 1874), p. 242.

[6] *Ibid.*, pp. 36–41.

[7] *Ibid.*, pp. 104–122. He here espouses Comte's religion of humanity, described in ch. 2, § III above.

[8] *Ibid.*, pp. 244–252, 257.

[9] *Essays Upon Controversial Questions* (D. Appleton-Century Company, Inc., New York, 1889), p. 183.

[10] *Hibbert Journal*, London, Vol. VI, 1908, p. 800.

[11] *The Philosophy of John Dewey* (ed. P. A. Schilpp, Northwestern University Press, Chicago, 1939), p. 596.

[12] A. J. Ayer, *Language, Truth, and Logic* (Gollancz, London, 1938), pp. 174, 175 and ch. VI in general.

[13] *The Demon of the Absolute* (Princeton University Press, Princeton, New Jersey, 1928), pp. 45, 46.

[14] *The Philosophy of John Dewey, loc. cit.*

[15] *Ibid.*, p. 597.

[16] *Language, Truth, and Logic*, p. 44.

[17] *The International Encyclopedia of Unified Science* (Chicago, 1938–    ) is devoted to this end, inspired by this creed, and written almost exclusively by pragmatists and logical positivists.

[18] For Mill's political and economic views, see his essay "On Liberty" which can be found in the Everyman edition of *Utilitarianism*.

[19] *Whither Mankind?* (ed. C. A. Beard, Longmans, Green & Co., Inc., New York, 1928), p. 67.

[20] *Ibid.*, p. 72.

[21] *Ibid.*, p. 65. Cf. Russell's *History of Western Philosophy*

(Simon and Schuster, Inc., New York, 1945), p. 827: "Dr. Dewey has an outlook which, where it is distinctive, is in harmony with the age of industrialism. . . . It is natural that his strongest appeal should be to Americans."

[22] *Knowledge for What?* (Princeton University Press, Princeton, New Jersey, 1939), p. 3.

[23] *Ibid.*, p. 99.

## Notes to Chapter 10

[1] "A Free Man's Worship," *Mysticism and Logic* (Allen & Unwin, London, 1917), pp. 47 ff.

[2] *The Works of Robert Louis Stevenson* (Jefferson Press, Boston, n.d.), Vol. II, pp. 595, 596.

[3] Job 28:12.

[4] *Science and the Modern World* (The Macmillan Company, New York, 1926), p. 24.

[5] T. S. Eliot, *Poems 1909–25* (Faber & Faber, London, 1936), pp. 123 ff.

[6] Quoted by Engels, *Socialism: Utopian and Scientific,* pp. 10 ff.

[7] *Ibid.*, pp. 13 ff.

[8] *The Fate of Man in the Modern World* (S. C. M. Press, London, 1935), p. 73.

[9] *Ibid.*, p. 77.

[10] *The Christian News-Letter,* Oxford, No. 289, pp. 6, 7.

[11] For the close interrelationship between science and its principles, the "scientific" tradition and its assumptions, Western secularism and its beliefs, and Marxist Communism and its dogmas, see the accompanying chart.

## Notes to Chapter 11

[1] N. Berdyaev, *Slavery and Freedom* (Charles Scribner's Sons, New York, 1944), p. 132.

[2] *Summa Contra Gentiles,* IV, 2, 2.

[3] The important works of Dilthey are not available in English. The best book on this philosopher is H. A. Hodges, *Wilhelm Dilthey, An Introduction* (Oxford University Press, New York, 1944). Reference to this book will show how much I am indebted to him on the question of the need for closer co-operation between the humanities and the sciences of man.

[4] Gen. 1:26.

[5] Gal. 4:3.

[6] W. Temple, *Nature, Man and God* (The Macmillan Company, London, 1935), p. 478.

[7] Gen. 1:31.

[8] Rev. 21:1, 2.

[9] Rom. 8:21.

[10] *Loc. cit.*

[11] Eph. 4:13.

[12] John 10:10.

[13] Ps. 107:30.

# INDEX

•

204

## Date Due

| | | | |
|---|---|---|---|
| APR 1 5 '62 | | | |
| JAN 1 9 '62 | | | |
| APR 1 7 '64 | | | |
| APR 9 '65 | | | |
| APR 3 0 '65 | | | |
| MAY 21 '65 | | | |
| | | | |
| | | | |
| | | | |
| | | | |
| | | | |
| | | | |
| | | | |
| | | | |
| | | | |
| | | | |
| | | | |
| | | | |
| GB | PRINTED | IN U. S. A. | |